# Research Methodology for Social and Legal Studies

**Edited by:**

- **Nathaniel Umukoro**
- **Florence Masajuwa**

# Research Methodology for Social and Legal Studies

Edited by:

- Nathaniel Umukoro
- Florence Masajuwa

Academica Press
Washington~London

Library of Congress Cataloging-in-Publication Data

Names: Umukoro, Nathanial (editor) | Masajuwa, Florence (editor)
Title: Research methodology for social and legal studies | Umukoro, Nathaniel | Masajuwa, Florence
Description: Washington : Academica Press, 2021. | Includes references.
Identifiers: LCCN 2021945442 | ISBN 9781680532692 (hardcover) | 9781680532708 (e-book)

# Contents

# CONTRIBUTORS

**Evelyn Osaretin-Ogbeide** is an Associate Professor in the Department of Economics, Edo State University, Uzairue.

**Olufemi Abifarin** is a Professor in the Faculty of Law, Federal University, Oye-Ekiti

**Joel A. Adeyeye** is a Lecturer in the Faculty of Law Kwara State University, Molete

**Omorede, Christiana Kayinwaye** is a Senior Lecturer in the Department of Public Administration, Faculty of the Social Sciences, University of Benin, Benin City

**Harrison Eromosele** is a Lecturer in the Department of Economics, Federal University, Otuoke

**Clement Odiri Obagbinoko** is a Lecturer in the Department of Political Science, Delta State University, Abraka

**Sylvester Ohiomu** is a Senior Lecturer in the Department of Economics and Development Studies, Igbinedion University, Okada

**Harriet Omokiniovo Efanodor-Obeten** is a Senior Lecturer in the Department of Political Science, Edo State University, Uzairue

**Anthony Iyoha Emhenya** is a Senior Lecturer in the Department of Political Science, Edo State University, Uzairue

**Peter Eshioke Egielewa** is a Lecturer in the Department of Mass Communication, Edo State University, Uzairue

**Florence Masajuwa** is an Associate Professor in the Faculty of Law, Edo State University, Uzairue

# CHAPTER ONE

# RESEARCH: CONCEPT, TYPES AND PROCESS

Evelyn Osaretin-Ogbeide

## The meaning of research

Research is a comprehensive study of issues of interest with the aim of getting a better understanding about the subject or the provision of new discovery and information which may be used for future research. According to Babbie (1998:2), research is a systematic inquiry with the aim of describing, explaining and predicting an observed phenomenon. Nordquist (2020:1) defined research as the collection and evaluation of information as regards a particular subject with the aim providing answer to the questions surrounding the study and generate new knowledge.

In social sciences, research is a careful and comprehensive study of a particular problem, concern, or issue using scientific method. It entails the gathering, analyzing and interpretation of information or data of different economic problems and activities with the aim of providing policies towards solving the problems. Neuman (2014), defined social science research as a careful observation of people and the environment using survey, experimental, or statistical tools to provide policy about their behaviour. Social science research is based on some rules and standard and these help to reduce misjudgment and bias from personal experience (Neuman, 2014). Most researches are based on data analysis and empirical investigation. These data and empirical analysis can be quantitative (using figures) or qualitative (using words, object and others).

**Characteristics of research**: all research are characterized by the following:

1. It has to do with a systematic approach, rules and procedures while making observations or drawing conclusions.
2. Research creates an avenue of generating new questions, giving room for more opportunities for research.
3. All research must be guided by accuracy. Data for the study must be accurate to achieve the desired objective.
4. Research is based on logical reasoning, involving either inductive and deductive methods or both.
5. The data gathered are given in-depth analysis to avoid any wrong conclusion

## Approaches to social science research

The approaches to research and research methods are the tools or instruments used to achieve the objective of the study. It depends on the objective of the study. *Themes and Variations,* (2014) noted that there is no single research approach suitable for all forms of study. However, choice of the approach to use in a research is a function of the question at hand. There are generally two approaches to research and they approaches both share major scientific principles, but differ in some ways. They have their strengths and limitations.

**Qualitative approach:** This approach is based only on inquiry to provide in-depth understanding of a particular problem or issue. It is the collection of information from different materials (Denzin and Lincoln, 2005). It focus on interactive processes and events and does not involve the application of statistical tools (Marvast, 2004). The outcome is highly dependent on the experience of the researchers and the questions used to probe the sample. It makes use of the following research tools in providing the understanding: One-to-one interview, Focus groups, and Ethnographic research, Content/Text Analysis or Case study research.

**Quantitative research:** this is a systematic way of collecting and analyzing data and drawing conclusions from the analyzed data. It measure objective facts about variables employing statistical processes and computation of the collect data. The data used in this type of research are numbers. The information are assigned numbers. Quantitative research usually deals with larger population. Data for this type of research are either primary or secondary. The primary data are gotten from surveys and questionnaires while the secondary data are from documented sources such as the Central Bank of Nigeria Statistical Bulletin, publication of National Bureau of Statistics, World Bank data etc (Denzin and Lincoln, 2003a).

**Other Approaches**

Schutt (2011) observed that other ways of classifying research types, methods and approaches are inductive and deductive. These however go hand in hand with the qualitative and quantitative research types:

**Inductive research methods**: this entails analyzing and observing activities/ events. It is mainly used for qualitative research where data are gathered using conversational methods of asking participants one-ended questions. The information gathered from the participants are not numerical. This method of research enables the researcher understand the views of the participants. Tools used here are:

- One-to-one Interview: one participant at time is attended to using this tool. The researcher prepares questions in advance and it is important to note here that only questions relevant to study should be asked. Inferences are drawn from the meaningful answers
- Focus Groups: these are small groups of around 6-10 participants who are experts in the subject matter with a moderator who facilitates the discussion. By asking correct questions, the moderator is able to collect information on the related research.
- Case Study: This the most valuable options for modern research used in the educational sector, philosophical studies, and psychological studies. This method involves a deep dive into ongoing research and collecting data.
- Ethnographic Research: This is an in-depth qualitative method of research where people are observed in their natural environment experiencing the normal setting and daily life of a group of people. It is demanding as researcher need to enter the natural environment of other people. There is also the challenge of geographic locations.
- Text Analysis: in this qualitative method/type of research, the researcher analyzes social constructs by decoding words through any available form of documentation. The researcher

studies and understands the context in which the documents are written with the aim of drawing meaningful inferences from it.

**Deductive methods**: this on the other hand has to do with verifying the observed events and goes hand in hand with quantitative research which is based on numbers and measurable forms. It begins with a theory and data collected and analyzed to prove the theory right or wrong It is usually used to answer questions with the objectives of justifying relationships with measurable variables to either explain, predict, or control a phenomenon.

In addition to the above, research can be classified as:

**Basic research: This type of research has to do with the collection of data** to enhance our knowledge. It is motivated by the need to expansion of knowledge with the aim of creating or inventing anything new. For example: an experiment to determine a simple fact.

**Applied research:** Applied research on the other hand focuses on analyzing and solving real-life problems. It involves the gathering and analyzing of data and applying the result to the real life problem of concern. For example: looking for a specific cure for a disease.

**Problem oriented and resolving research:** this type of research is concerned with understanding the exact nature of a problem and providing solutions to problems. For example, assume the revenue of a biscuit company has decreased by 10% in the last year. The company will be interested to know why and the probable areas to question could be the quality of the product, activities of competitors, economic situation (fall in income, etc). The findings from research are used in solving the problems. For instance, if from our above question of the fall in revenue and it was discovered that the activities of the competitors are the major cause of the fall in revenue, the biscuit company can apply other forms of customer attracting incentives.

## Research process

All research work must beginning with a problem of concern which is usually turned into a question and choosing an appropriate method to investigate the problem. The problem has to do with what the researcher really intends to find out. The problem may arise from a former research, literatures or observing the surrounding. Research question must be answerable and should not be vague otherwise, there is no research (Stebbins, 2006). All research follow some sequence of steps and these steps differs based on the approach to be used. Hence, we will be discussing the general procedures for research as well as the slight differences with different approaches to research.

The following are the general process in conducting a research:

Step 1: The identification and formulation of research problem: this is the first step in research. If there is no problem, there will not be research since research is basically the act of seeking solution to a problem. "A research problem is a definite/clear expression ot statement about an area of concern, a condition to be improved upon, a difficulty to be eliminated, or a troubling question in scholarly literature, in theory, or within practice that requires meaningful understanding and deliberate investigation" (Guba and Yvonna, 1994). The research problem which is based on the area of interest of the researcher can come from previous research, proving the validity of an existing theory or the conditions around the topic of study. The research problem leads to the formulation of the research question. The formulation of research question makes the objective of the researcher clear. It gives a guide to the researcher. The formulation of research question is guided by:

1. What the researcher wants' to know?
2. Why the researcher is interested in knowing what he/she seeks to know and seeking answers to the particular questions?
3. What are the probable answers to the questions?

Step 2: Formulation of hypothesis: This is the formulation of a tentative explanation of the problem in the form of a proposition wherever feasible. This is the conjectural statement of the relation between two or more variables; the dependent variable and independent variable(s) and its tenability is often tested. Information from different sources (previous theories, and research works) are put together. The research hypothesis is usually a prediction derived from theory which is to be test. It is stated mostly in the null form which states that there is no relationship between/the variables in the study or impact.

However, not all studies begin with clear formulation of hypothesis. While some studies are hypothesis testing others are hypothesis formulating such as exploratory studies as the researcher ends up formatting hypothesis from the study.

Step 3: The review of relevant literatures: since most research are based on previous knowledge, the researcher takes the second step after the identification of the problem to reading documentations that are related to the research problem. This provides the researcher more information, a direction and knowledge to determine the gap that exists in previous studies to avoid duplication of previous findings. It also helps the researcher to know how the question can be answered, providing information on the tools to be used in answering the question as well as the source data and method of collecting data. Review of relevant literature also requires the analysis of the summary of the writings of earlier researches in the area of study.

Literature review can be theoretical or empirical literature. Theoretical literatures are literatures that has not been subjected to data analysis before the conclusion is drawn. They are formulated from observations. Empirical literatures are documentations of the studies and findings as a result of relevant data being subjected to different form of analysis. Some of the sources of literature are text books; official publications (Central Bank, World Bank, etc)

Step 4: Research design/Methodology: having identified the problem, formulated the hypothesis from the problem and had reviewed relevant literature, the researcher proceeds to looking for how the problem can be solved. A research design is the general framework for the collection, measurement and analyzing of data. The research design/methodology helps in the validity of the research objectively, accurately and economically and thereby ensures against its failure. It also includes in identifying the target population which is for the results of research is needed for and the sample which is a subset of the population. Samples can be drawn based on Probability sampling (based on scientific technique), purposive/subjective/judgment sampling (drawn deliberately or purposely based on the objectives of the study), and mixed sampling (sampled based partly on probability on fixed sampling). Some general types of sampling are: Simple random sampling. Complex random sampling, Stratified random sampling. Cluster and area sampling, haphazard or convenience sampling, quota sampling, judgment sampling etc.

These however, varies according to the research purposes which can be: Exploration, Description, Diagnosis and Experimentation.

The research design/methodology can follow the following steps:

1. Sampling design which concerns with describing the different sampling methods to be used for selection of units for study.
2. Observational design which describes the way in which the observations are to be made.
3. Statistical design where applicable which deals with the statistical techniques to be applied in the analysis and interpretation of data.
4. Operational design which incorporates all the three steps above.

Step 5: Data collection: sources data for research can be secondary or primary or secondary sources and this is based on the objective of the study, the scope of the study, the type of research and the method/approach of the research. Secondary data are collected from books, publications and report of previous studies, documentation of government official etc. primary data on the other hand are collected from experiment or surveys. Survey data may be gathered from observation, interviews (telephonic or personal), questionnaires, etc.

Step 6: Data analysis: the data collected is analyzed. Data analysis is the process of collecting and organizing data with the aim of drawing inference. Data analysis can be qualitative and quantitative. Qualitative methods among others include, content analysis, narrative analysis, and discourse analysis. Qualitative analysis is the common method and used in analyzing documented information such as text or media which depends on the nature of the research questions. It is used to analyze the responses from interview. The narrative method on the other hand is uses stories experiences shared by people in answering the research questions.

The quantitative methods of analysis data makes use of quantitative variables which can be discrete (such as height, age) or continuous (number of students in a class). The data for the variable are analyzed using the descriptive and inferential statistics. The descriptive statistics is the first stage of quantitative method of analysis. It helps in summarizing the data to determine the patterns of the data presenting absolute figures. It however do not provide the rationale for those numbers and not used for generalization. It is used in analyzing single analysis hence, they are called univariate analysis. It makes use of tools such:

- Mean: this is the average of the set of data for the variable. E.g the mean age of students in a class.
- Median: this shows the midpoint of a set of numerical values.
- Mode: most common value in the midst of the data for the variable. E.g the mode of the ages of the students in a class.
- Percentage: employed in expressing how a value or group of respondents within the data relates to a larger group of respondents.
- Frequency: the number of times a value is found.
- Range: the highest and lowest value in a set of values.

  The inferential statistics on the other hand are used to show the relationship among multiple of variables with the aim of generalizing and making predictions. Statisticians have developed programs like SPSS or STATA or even Excel for the calculation of the different tools for inferential statistics. Among tools for inferential statistics are:

- Correlation: this shows the relationship between two variables. When the two variables are moving in same direction (each increasing), there is positive correlation and is in opposite direction, there is negative correlation, the correlation is determined by the correlation coefficient (R/r) using some tools such as spearman's correlation coefficient, the rank correlations. It lies between -1 and 1. The closer it is to 0 the lower the relationship between the variables.
- Regression: this predicts or shows the relationship between two variables. It is a step higher than the correlation. Regression analysis is a set of statistical methods that are used in the estimation of the relationship between the dependent variable and the independent variable(s). E.g the impacts of age and gender on the performance of a student in a class. Regression analysis can be linear simple, linear multiple or no-linear. Linear simple is the most common and stated as: The equation

is given as :Y= a + bX, where Y is the dependent variable and X is the independent variable. b is the slope of the line and a is the y-intercept.

- Analysis of variance: this test the extent to which two or more groups differ. The ANOVA (one-way or two-ways) are used in this analysis. The F-test is also used here.

Step 7: interpretation, Hypothesis testing and generalization: the result from the data analyzed is interpreted. The findings are explained based on the basis of some theoretical framework. This may probably raise some new questions for further researches. The result is also used in testing the hypothesis where applicable. A stronger test of argument is formed when the null hypothesis is rejected and the alternative hypothesis which is the opposite of the null is accepted which is the operational statement of the researcher's research hypothesis. In social science, the decision to accept or reject the null hypothesis is tested based on 0.05 or .01 alpha level of significance. Generalization is made on this finding. Some statistical tool for testing the hypothesis are the F-test, t-test or the chi-square test. The Chi Square statistic is commonly used to test the relationships between categorical variables or to determine whether there is a statistically significant difference between the expected frequencies and the observed frequencies in one or more categories of a contingency table. It is given as:

$$\chi^2 = \Sigma \frac{(O-E)^2}{E}$$

However, where there is no hypothesis in the study, generalization is just made from the result of which further studies can be carried on.

Step 8: Recommendation: the main aim of research is the formulation of policy or make recommendation. The theory or background upon which the research is being carried out and result found is supported or rejected and recommendations are made on what need to be done to bring solution to the problem of the study. Recommendations can also be made for more studies to be carried out on the topic.

These above steps discussed above may have slight difference for the two major types of research (qualitative and quantitative) and the research question of the study. While the steps discussed above are more of the steps for a quantitative research, the qualitative research tend to take follow steps:

Step 1-2: Acknowledging self and context: This has to do with the researcher relying on personal beliefs of specific current issues from which the topic of the study is drawn. From here, inquiry is placed on the context of the discussion with some other researchers.

**3–6.** Design a study and collect, analyze, and interpret data: Like that of quantitative research, the design of the study is carried out, data collected, analyzed and interpreted. In most cases, past theories are tested as well as new ones being built.

**7.** Recommendation: This is same for both quantitative and qualitative method but the style of a report will vary based on the approach used.

The figures 1 and 2 shows the differences in the research process for the quantitative and qualitative method of research.

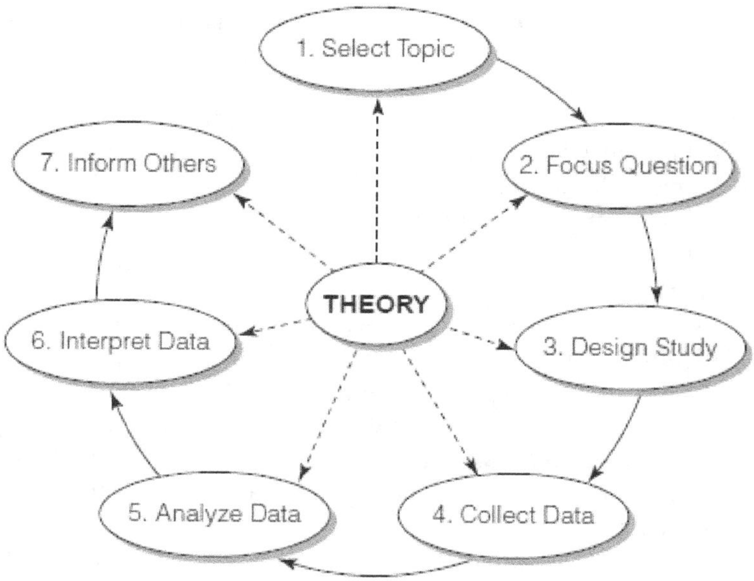


**FIGURE 1 Steps in the Quantitative Research Process**

**Source: Neuman, 2014**

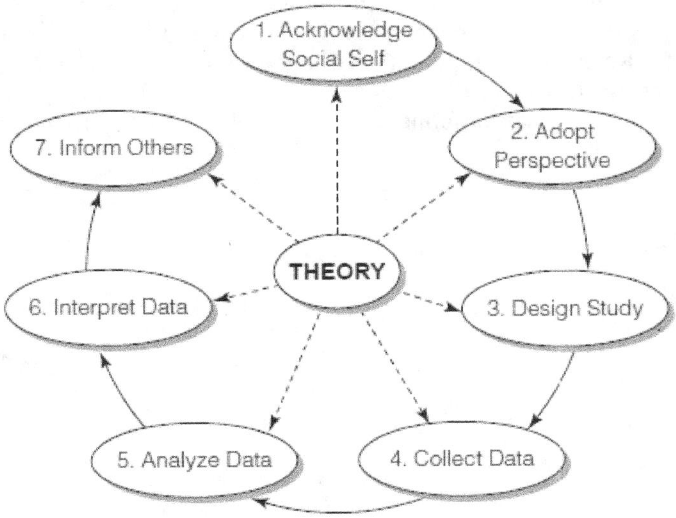


**FIGURE 2 Steps in the Qualitative Research Process**

**Source: Neuman, 2014**

## References

Babbie (1998).The Practice of Social Research Wadsworth Publishing Company, Amazon .com. retrieved from https://books.google.com.ng/books/about/The_Practice_of_Social_Research.html?id=q_F9AAAAIAAJ&redir_esc=y

Denzin and Lincoln, Eds (2003a). Collecting and interpreting qualitative material. 2nd Eds. • Thousand Oaks CA: SAGE Publications London

Denzin, N. K & Lincoln, Y (2005). The Handbook of Qualitative Research, 3rd edition. SAGE Thousand Oaks, CA: Sage,

Guba, E. G., and Lincoln, Y. S. "Competing Paradigms in Qualitative Research." In *Handbook of Qualitative Research*. Norman K. Denzin and Yvonna S. Lincoln, editors. (Thousand Oaks, CA: Sage, 1994), pp. 105-117.

Marvast, A. B. (2004), Qualitative Research in Sociology. An Introduction. SAGE Publications London • Thousand Oaks • New Delhi Pp 7-8

Neuman, L. W. (2014). Social Research Methods: Qualitative and Quantitative Approaches, Pearson international edition, 7th edition Education Limited Edinburgh Gate Harlow

Nordquist, R. (2020). Research in Essays and Reports. ThoughtCo. Retrieved from thoughtco.com/research-essays-and-reports-1692048.

Schutt, R. (2011). Investigating the Social World: The Process and Practice of Research, 7th Edition, SAGE Publications, Inc.

Stebbins, L.F (2006). *Student Guide to Research in the Digital Age*. How to locate and evaluate information sources, Westport CT Libraries Unlimited, 2006).

# CHAPTER TWO

# A CRITICAL ANALYSIS OF LEGAL RESEARCH METHODOLOGY

**Olufemi Abifarin and Joel A. Adeyeye**

## Introduction

Research is defined as a systematic search for facts or scientific investigation of the principles and facts of any subject based on original and first hand study authorities or experiments (Ayua, 1983). It involves searching into the matter closely and carefully. It is an inquiry directed at the discovery of truth (Worthly, 1983). It should be noted that research is an activity that is essentially in the public domain (Bak, 2004).

These kinds of issues that are being researched, the way in which they are addressed and investigated, and the dissemination of the findings, are all embedded in shared practices of the discipline in which you will be working (Bak, 2004). One can however classify legal research into doctrinal and non-doctrinal.

## Doctrinal Legal research

### Introduction

Doctrinal legal research, as conceived in the legal research domain, is research 'about' what the prevailing state of legal doctrine, legal rule, or legal principle is. A legal scholar undertaking doctrinal legal research, therefore, takes one or more legal propositions, principles, rules or doctrines as a starting point and focus of his study. He 'locates' such a principle, rule or doctrine in statutory instrument(s), judicial opinions thereon, discussions thereof in legal treatises, commentaries, textbooks, encyclopedias: legal periodicals, and debates, if any, that took place at the formative stage of such a rule, doctrine or proposition. Thereafter, he 'reads' them in a holistic manner and makes an 'analysis' of the material as well as of the rules, doctrines and formulates his 'conclusions' and writes up his study. For example, a legal researcher interested in criminal law might start with proposition dealing with right against self-incrimination. Research then takes place in the law library, where he Will 'locate' the proposition (along with its different contours) and its discussions in treatises and textbooks on criminal law, criminal procedure, and constitutional law, encyclopedia and leading legal periodicals. He will also try to locate all relevant judicial pronouncements of the higher judicial institutions delved into the right against self-incrimination. He will then 'read' these materials and 'analyze' them by applying his power of reasoning and Will, premised on analytical perspective and the material used, draw some conclusions about the proposition. He then will write up his Study. He may, in his study advance a set of formulations, supportive or otherwise, with convincing 'reasoning' about the proposition-the right against self-incrimination. He, in his research report, may offer an alternative comprehensive paradigm of the doctrine. With a view to drawing parallels between the doctrine or rule under inquiry, he may also find a comparable doctrine or rule from other jurisdictions. He may, depending upon 'objectives' of his research, also propose a new formulation of the rule or doctrine, a model statute or a statutory provision. He may also highlight the purpose and policy of law that exist and may propose what it ought to be (Taiwo, 2011).

Doctrinal legal research, thus, involves: (i) systematic analysis of statutory provisions and of legal principles involved therein, or derived there from, and (ii) logical and rational ordering of the legal propositions and principles.

Doctrinal legal research, in addition to analytical one, may be historical or comparative (Bak, 2004). Historical legal research, unlike analytical one, deals with the past. It throws light on the past to understand the present. It explores the circumstances that led to the adoption of the existing law. It gives a clue to the reasons why a particular provision of law or law was framed in the form in which now it appears. It also often reveals that a particular existing provision/

law, fully justifiable at the time when it was introduced, is no longer justifiable because the reasons/circumstances that justified the original inclusion of that provision/law are no longer valid. While comparative legal research, as evident from its title, involves comparative study of comparable laws or legal institutions from different jurisdictions. It exhibits the lessons that can be learnt from each other's failures and achievements.

### Aims of Doctrinal Legal Research

According to (Taiwo, 2011) Doctrinal legal research:

1. aims to study case law and statutory law, with a view to find law,
2. aims at consistency and certainty of law,
3. (to some extent) looks into the purpose and policy of law that exists, and
4. aims to study legal institutions.

### Basic tools of Doctrinal Legal Research

The basic tools of a doctrinal legal researcher, thus, are: (i) statutory materials, (ii) case reports, (iii) standard textbooks and reference books, (iv) legal_periodicals, (v) Parliamentary Debates and Government Reports, and (Vi) Micro films and CD-ROM.

#### i. Statutory materials

Legislative Acts constitute one of the basic tools of doctrinal legal research. However, a plethora of subsidiary or secondary legislation in the form of rules, regulations, byelaws, notifications, statutory orders or directives is found in the modern national legal system. In fact, in a contemporary legal system the quantum of executive legislative instruments overweighs the primary ones, (Kok, 2002).

#### ii. Case reports

In almost all the common law legal systems, judicial decisions of higher courts are published in Case Reports. A doctrinal legal researcher, therefore, has to look for the apt Case Reports for laying his hands on the required judicial pronouncements for his analysis.

### iii. Legal periodicals

It may also be necessary for a doctrinal legal researcher to know What others have said and found in the area of his research. Therefore, he is required to look into research articles published in legal periodicals of repute.

### Advantages of Doctrinal Legal Research

According to (Gasiokwu, 2001), Doctrinal legal research has a number of advantages to its credit. A few pertinent among them are outlined here below.

*First*, doctrinal legal research, which basically involves analysis of legal principles, concepts or doctrines, their logical ordering and systematizing of legal propositions emerging there from, has some practical utility. It provides quick answers to the problem as the researcher is continuously engaged in the exposition and analysis of legislation and case-law and the integration of statutory provisions and judicial pronouncements into a coherent and workable body of doctrine.

*Secondly,* a doctrinal legal researcher, through his analysis, attempts to test the logical coherence, consistency and technical soundness of a legal proposition or doctrine.

*Thirdly,* doctrinal legal research contributes in our understanding of 'law,' legal concept or doctrine, and legal processes in a better way as it Offers logical exposition and analysis of such a law or a doctrine or legal system. Such an analysis also reveals (in) consistency in, and (un)certainty of, the law, legal principles or doctrines.

*Fourthly,* a scholar of law indulged in doctrinal legal research, in a systematic way and with convincing reasoning, exhibits 'inbuilt' 'loopholes,' 'gaps,' 'ambiguities' or 'inconsistencies' in the substantive law inquired into as well as in some of principles or doctrines embodied therein.

*Fifthly,* a doctrinal legal researcher, through logical ordering and systematizing of legal propositions that emerged from his analysis and reasoning may initiate a theory in the concerned field of law.

## Limitations

Doctrinal legal research, in spite of the above-mentioned strengths, suffers from certain limitations of worth noting. They are: First, analysis of the legal principle, doctrine under inquiry, in particular, and of 'law' in general, and the consequential projections of the doctrinal researcher, ultimately, become 'subjective' and exhibit his 'perception' about the inquired subject-matter. A different perception of the same legal principle, concept, doctrine or law by another scholar(s) of law, therefore, cannot be ruled out.

*Secondly,* a doctrinal legal researcher gathers the policy from his own experience, authoritative statutory materials, case reports, and his reflections thereon. His 'inquiry' into a legal principle or concept or law, therefore, does not get any Support from social facts or values. His research, undeniably, becomes merely theoretical and devoid of any social facts. Consequently, his 'projections' of law and 'predictions' regarding changes in the law are bound to be far from social reality and inadequate.

*Thirdly,* doctrinal legal research does not involve a study of the factors that lie outside law or legal system but have directly or indirectly influenced the operation of the law, a legal rule, concept or doctrine.

*Fourthly,* a doctrinal legal researcher puts his sole reliance on, and gives prominence to, traditional sources of law and judicial pronouncements of appellate courts. The actual practice and attitude of lower courts and of administrative agencies with quasi-judicial powers, whose judgments remain unreported, are left unexplored in doctrinal legal research.

## Non-Doctrinal Legal Research Or Social-Legal Research

In the recent past, doctrinal legal research has received a severe jolt due to change in the political philosophy of law from the *laissez faire* to the welfare state envisaging socioeconomic transformation through law and legal institutions, the consequential new substantive and functional facets of law, and certain compelling pragmatic considerations arising from this metamorphosis.

Prominent reasons and arguments stressing the need for inquiry into social facets of law are: *First,* the emergence of sociological jurisprudence (Pound, 1979) and its underlying philosophy assigned 'law' the task of 'social engineering.' Almost every modern civilized State perceives 'law' as an active instrument of socio-economic justice and thereby a vehicle of social engineering. This new operational facet of law has inevitably led to enactment of enormous statutes with specified socio-economic drives. In fact, we have come to live in an age is of social welfare laws. *Secondly,* in the light of such a role assigned to law, it is argued, it becomes necessary to look into the 'factors' or 'interests' of the Legislature that play significant role in setting the legislative process in motion and in identifying the beneficiaries thereof and the reasons therefor. These 'factors' and 'interests' (for putting law in motion for the desired planned socio-economic change), indicate, rather dictate, 'framework' of the law as well reveal the choices opted by the Legislature When it faced with alternative 'paths' towards, or 'strategies' for, the intended legislative goal. *Thirdly,* it becomes necessary to carry out frequent attitudinal studies of those whose legal position is sought to be modified by a given law as well as of those who are vested with the power of interpreting and implementing it so that the Legislature, armed with this feedback, can fulfill its job in a more satisfactory manner. Fourthly, a number of facts or factors that lie outside a legal system may be responsible for non-implementation or poor implementation of a given piece 6f social legislation. A systematic probe into these factors and their influence on the operation of law, therefore, becomes necessary to identify these bottlenecks and to design appropriate strategy to remove them or to minimize their influence on the law so that the law can be made an effective instrument of socio-economic transformation. *Fifthly,* there is nearly always a certain 'gap' between actual social behavior and the behavior demanded by the legal norm and certain 'tension' between actual behavior and legally desired behavior. Identification of the 'gap' and 'tension' as Well as factors responsible therefor becomes necessary for strengthening potentials of law as a vehicle for socio-economic justice, (Aboki, 2001).

## Aims of Non-Doctrinal Legal Research

The researcher tries primarily to seek, among other things, answers to:

1. Are laws and legal institutions serving the needs of society?
2. Are they suited to the society in which they are operating?
3. What forces in society have influenced shaping or reshaping a particular set of laws or legal norms?
4. Are laws properly administered and enforced or do they exist only in statute books?
5. What are the factors, if any, responsible for poor or non-implementation of the laws?
6. What are the factors that influenced the adjudicators (courts or administrative agencies) in interpreting and administrating the laws?
7. For whose benefit a law is enacted, and are they using it? Has the intended 'legislative targets' benefited from the law? If not, for what reasons? Where do 'bottlenecks' lie? What has been impact of the: law or legal institutions in changing attitude of the people or molding their behavior? What are the social obstacles in realization of the expected behavior or change? (Aboki, 2001).

## Basic tools of Non-Doctrinal Legal Research

The basic tools of data collection for a socio-legal research, thus, are: (i) interview, (ii) questionnaire, (iii) schedule, (iv) interview guide, (v) observation, participant or non-participant, and (vi) published or unpublished materials (such as Census Reports, Reports of Governmental and / or Non-Governmental Agencies, and appropriate literature on sociology of law).

## Advantages of Non-Doctrinal Legal Research

A few prominent advantages are:

*First,* social-legal research highlights the 'gaps' between 'legislative goals' and 'social reality' and thereby 'depicts' a 'true picture' of 'law-in-action.' It particularly highlights the 'gap' in relation to (a) the practice of law enforcers, regulators and adjudicators and (b) the use or under-use of the law by intended beneficiaries of the law.

*Secondly,* non-doctrinal legal research carries significance in the modern welfare state, which envisages socio-economic transformation through law and thereby perceives law as a means of achieving socio-economic justice and parity. Through empiricism, socio-legal research assesses 'role and contribution of law' in bringing the intended social consequences. It also helps us in assessing 'impact of law' on the social values, outlook, and attitude towards the 'change(s)' contemplated by law under inquiry. It highlights the 'factors' that have been creating 'impediments' or posing 'problems' for the law in attaining its 'goal(s).'

*Thirdly,* in continuity of what has been said in firstly and secondly above, non-doctrinal legal research provides an 'expert advice' and gives significant feedback to the policy-makers, Legislature, and Judges for better formulation, enforcement and interpretation of the law.

*Fourthly,* socio-legal research renders an invaluable help in 'shaping' social legislations in tune with the social engineering philosophy of the modern state and in 'making' them more effective instruments of the planned socio-economic transformation, (Aboki, 2001).

## Limitations of Non-Doctrinal Legal Research

Though socio-legal research has great potentials, yet a few limitations (Jain, 1974) thereof need to mention here to put its role in the right perspective. A few significant are outlined below.

*First,* non-doctrinal legal research is extremely time consuming and costly as it requires a lot of time for collecting the required information from field. Further, it calls for additional training in designing and employing tools of data collection and entails greater commitments of time and energy to produce meaningful results, either for policy-makers or theory-builders, (International Law Centre NY 1974). *Secondly*, socio-legal research, as explained earlier, needs a strong base of doctrinal legal research. A legal scholar who is weak in doctrinal legal research cannot handle non-doctrinal legal research in a meaningful way. It may turn out to be a futile exercise leading to no significant results.

*Thirdly,* the basic tools of data collection, namely interview, questionnaire, schedule and observation, are not simple to employ. They require specialized knowledge and skill from the stage of planning to execution. Each one of them is bridled with a number of difficulties, (International Law Centre New York 1974).

*Fourthly,* invariably public opinion, as mentioned earlier, influences contents and framework of law. Law, most of the times, also seeks to mould and/or change the public opinion, social value and attitude. Fifthly, sometimes, because of complicated social, political and economic settings and varied multiple factors a socio-legal researcher may again be thrown back to his own ideas, prejudices and feelings in furnishing solutions to certain problems. *Sixthly,* Socio-legal research becomes inadequate and inapt where the problems are to be solved and the law is to be developed from case to case (like in administrative law and law of torts).

## Conclusion

Doctrinal legal research, for a variety of reasons, plausibly including the inability and inaptitude of legal scholars to undertake socio-legal research, has been (and is still) prominent in the field of law. Since its evolution, law has been viewed as a science of norms and a 'closed discipline.' Hence, scholars of law have been endeavoring to look into normative character of 'law' and the 'principles' involved therein through analysis of 'statutory' law. Analytical positivism has obsessed the thinking 0f Bar, Bench and academicians to such an extent that no other approach (other than doctrinal one) to the understanding of the nature and purpose of law could really have thrived.

## Bibliography

Aboki, Yusuf., Introduction to Legal Research Methodology (tamaza Publishing Co. Ltd, Zaria, 2001).

Adewale Taiwo., Basic Concepts in Legal Research Methodology (St Paul Publishing House Ibadan, 201 1).

Ayua, I.A., "Legal Research and Development" in Ayua, LA. 85 Guobadia, D.A. (eds), Law and Research Methodology. (NIALS, Lagos, 2001).

Bak, N., Completing Your Thesis: A practical Guide (Van Schaik Publishers, Pretoria, 2004).

Gasiokwu, M.O.U., "Legal Research and Development" in Ayua, LA. 8:. Guobadia, D.A. (eds), Law and Research Methodology (NIALS, Lagos, 2001).

International Legal Center for Law in Development (Research Advisory Committee on Law and Development), Report on Law and Development 10 (New York, 1974).

kok, A., Nienaber, A, 85 Viljoel, F., Skills Workbook for Students (Juta Law, 2002).

Worthley, B.A., “Some Reflections on Legal Research. after Thirty Years” Silver Jubilee of the Indian Law Institute Publication No. 7, Legal Research Methodology (1983).

# CHAPTER THREE
# RESEARCH DESIGN

**Omorede, Christiana Kayinwaye**

## Introduction

Research design is not a new phenomenon. The term is commonly used and also generally misunderstood particularly by emerging researchers. Research design is a very important component of research writing at all levels. This chapter is focused on "Research Design." While the discussions in this chapter may not be exhaustive, it would serve as a guide for research design in social sciences and law among others. The chapter takes a cursory look at the meaning of research and design. The chapter further explains the concept of research design, and also explicates its purpose as well as elaborate on various types of research design. The origin of research design as a recognized field of study is traceable to the 1960s after a conference on design methods at Imperial College London.

To understand the concept Research Design, it is pertinent to beam some light on the terminologies "research" and "design."

## What Is Research?

Research is a familiar word to post-graduate or Ph. D students as well as science loving individuals. Sometimes research and science are used synonymously as same thing. It is important to note that it is through researches that scientific discoveries are made (new discoveries are usually the products of research). For example the vaccine for the New Corona Virus (COVID-19) is currently going through series of researches. A vaccine can only emerge through the help of long and efficient research. In like manner research is also applicable in other academic disciplines aside the medical science to arrive at new or improved ways of doing things. Research is a vital part of the development and discoveries of new things in all academic subjects. From science to Public Administration and from public administration in social sciences to Law, every subject now has some kind of research work in it.

A number of definitions of research have been proposed by different scholars and writers in different fields. The Oxford Advanced Learners 'Dictionary' of Current English (1986) defines research as a "systematic investigation undertaken in order to discover new facts and get additional information." Saunders, Lewis and Thornhill (2003) in White (2019) describe research as "something that people undertake in order to find out new things in a systematic way, thereby increasing their knowledge." Research is described as systematic because the inquiry is usually on a specific topic that searches into the topic in a logical way to arrive at verifiable decisions. This is done in a manner that ensures that data obtained can be generalized, such that it can be applied to a wider range of situations than the one studied, and that the data are not influenced by the conscious or unconscious bias of the investigator or by any other extraneous factors. It equally involves validating or invalidating existing facts, theories, laws, models, paradigms and approaches. A researcher may decide to complement the works of other scholars or begin a fresh study with the aim of solving identified problems. In other words, research is a systematic, coherent and sequential way of data collection, analysis and interpretation with a view to making dependable conclusion and useful recommendations (Ujo, 2004).

From the definitions of research provided above, it follows that research is an intended activity, meant to create new evidences and facts about a particular phenomenon. It is in the light of the numerous benefits inherent in research undertakings that the field of management and social sciences The research process encompasses the identification of a specific problem or area of concern, interpreting that problem into a research problem, collecting data, analyzing the data and reporting the findings of the research. In other words one can say that research is a strategic and an organized activity carried out with an intention to ascertain new facts or at the identification of relationships among facts.

Research is necessary to researchers /students because it helps them to inquire about things that are said and done, rather than accepting or rejecting them at face value. Research helps to gather evidence for things that are said and done before making decisions. With research, decisions are based on evidence not on some sort of guesses. This is because through research, evidence is gathered in ways that minimize bias, since alternatives are considered before decisions are made. One can therefore evaluate things that are said and done from the weaknesses and strengths of those arguments or events. This subsequently increases the chances that decisions reached are going to be helpful and realistic in solving problems. It is in the light of the numerous benefits inherent in research undertakings that the field of social sciences and law considered research as one of their core subjects.

## Defining Design

The word design is often used as a generic term that refers to anything that was made by a conscious human effort. A design is a plan or specification for the erection of an object or system or for the implementation of an activity or a procedure or the result of that plan or specification in the form of a prototype, product or process. According to Hardt (2006) different countries have their concept of the word design. For Denmark, the term "design is to design the design of a design." For Swedish, design is defined as the planned and innovative use of available knowledge to form processes, environment, products and services with point of departure in users' needs. He further elaborated on the various definitions of the word design by different countries. The definitions of the concept above indicate that the word design is complex. However the commonality in the various definitions show that to design is to devise courses of action aimed at changing existing situations into preferred ones. As a process design is used to systematically solve problems. So a design process is a systematic problem solving strategy, with criteria and constraints, used to develop many possible solutions to solve or satisfy human needs or wants and to narrow down the possible solutions to one final choice

## The Concept of Research Design

Research design refers to the overall strategy that a researcher selects in incorporating the diverse components of the study in an articulate and consistent manner, to ensure that he/she effectively addresses the research problem. It is the conceptual blueprint within which research is conducted. Before a researcher embarks on a study s/he prepares an action plan, which constitutes the outline of collection, measurement and analysis of data. Research design is not associated to any particular technique of data collection or any particular type of data. When designing research it is necessary that we recognize the type of evidence required to answer the research question(s) in a reasonable way. Various authors have defined research design from different perspectives.

Leedy (1997:195) defines research design as a plan for a study, providing the overall framework for collecting data. MacMillan and Schumacher (2001:166) on their part define it as a plan for selecting subjects, research sites, and data collection procedures to answer the research question(s). They further indicate that the goal of a sound research design is to provide results that are judged to be credible. For Durrham (2004:29) research design is a strategic framework for action that serves as a bridge between research questions and the execution or the implementation of the research strategy. Green and Tull (1970) are of the view that research design is the specification of methods and procedures for acquiring the information needed. It is the overall operational pattern or framework of the project that stipulates what information is to be collected from which sources by what procedures.

Miller emphasis on designed research is the planned sequence of the entire process involved in conducting a research study. According to P. V. Young, "Research design is the logical and systematic planning and directing of a piece of research." Selltiz and others in Akhtar (2016) define research design as a "catalogue of the various phases and facts relating to the formulation of a research effort. It is an arrangement of the essential conditions for collection and analysis of data in a form that aims to combine relevance to research purpose with economy with a procedure." In the words of Ackoff "Design is the process of making decisions before the situation arises in which the decision has to be carried out. It is a process of deliberate anticipation directed towards bringing an unexpected situation under control." E. A. Suchman says that "a research design represents a compromise directed by many practical considerations that go into social research." He says further "a research design is not a highly specific plan to be followed without deviation, but rather a series of guide posts to keep one headed in the right direction." According to Jahoda, Deutsch and Cook, in Akhatar (2016) "a research design is the arrangement of conditions for collection and analysis of data in a manner that aims to combine relevance to the research purpose with economy in procedure." Therefore, the best study design should be repeatable, generalizable etc, which gives more reliability to the study.

Akhtar on his part opined that research design can be considered as the structure of research it is the "Glue" that holds all of the elements in a research project together, in short it is a plan of the proposed research work.

Creswell and Creswell (2018:11) define research design as "types of inquiry within qualitative, quantitative and mixed methods approaches that provides specific direction for procedures in a research study." For Bryman (2016) research design provides a "framework for the collection and analysis of data," and can be both within quantitative and qualitative research strategies. Therefore Bryman categorized research design into experimental, cross-sectional, longitudinal, cross study, and comparative. All of them can be used in both quantitative and qualitative research strategies.

It can further be analyzed from Alvin and Roland (2003) perspective that research design is a set of advanced decisions that make up the master plan specifying the methods and procedures for collecting and analyzing the needed information. While David J. Luck and Roland Rubin, emphasized the point that "a research design is the determination and statement of the general research approach or strategy adopted/or the particular project which ensures that the client's needs will be served." From the various definitions and contributions of authors proposed above it is no gain saying that preparing the research design is a very necessary stage in the process of conducting a research study. From the foregoing it is essential to note that a research design is the basic plan that guides the data collection and analysis phase of the research project. It provides the framework, or structure that specifies the type of information to be collected, its sources and collection procedure, without which a research report cannot be adequately presented. It implies the overall scheme or program of the research embracing an outline of what the researcher intends to do, ranging from the stage of formulation of hypothesis and their working implications to the final stage of data analysis. Kinnear and Taylor, (1996), Churchill and Iacobucci, (2005) "identify research design as the blueprint that is followed to complete the study and it ensures that the study is relevant to the problem and uses economical procedure." It is a more abstracted way of schematizing a process, so your strategy could be generalized to solve similar problems in other fields.

It is often argued that if the study is not completed within the time limit, it will not only increase the cost but also cause a series of other problems associated with research, affecting the quality of research. Therefore, "the challenge of a research is to translate the general scientific model into a practical research operation. Research design thus refers to the entire process of planning and carrying out a research study." It involves the arrangement of conditions and observations in such a way that alternative answers to the questions taken up in the research are ruled out, containing a built in system of checks against all the factors that might affect the validity of the research outcome.

## The Importance of Research Design

Research design is important as it prepares proper framework within which the researcher's work/activity will be actually carried out. Research design acts as a blue print for the conduct of the whole research project. It deals with the logical problem and not the logistical problem (Yin, 1989). In social science the issue of sampling, methods of data collection such as (questionnaire, observation, document analysis, and design questions) are all subsidiary to the matter of what evidence the researcher needs to collect. It introduces efficiency in investigation and generates confidence in the final outcome of the study. Research design gives proper direction and time-table to research activity. It keeps adequate checks on the research work and ensures it completion within time limit. It keeps the whole research project on the right track.

Research avoids possible errors as regards research problem, information requirement and so on. It gives practical orientation to the whole research work and makes it relevant to the marketing problems faced by the sponsoring organization. Finally, it makes the whole research process compact and result –oriented. A researcher should not go ahead with his project unless the research design is planned properly.

The function of research design is to ensure that requisite data in accordance with the problem at hand is collected accurately and economically. Simply stated, it is the framework, a blueprint for the research study which guides the collection and analysis of data. The research design depending upon the needs of the researcher may be a very detailed statement or only furnish minimum information required for planning the research project. To be effective, a research design should provide at least the following details;

- A statement of objectives of the study or the study output
- A statement of the data inputs required on the basis of which the research problem is to be solved.
- The methods of analysis which shall be used to treat and analysis the data inputs.

Research design has a significant impact on the reliability of the results obtained. It thus acts as a firm foundation for the entire research. It stands for advance planning of the methods to be adopted for collecting the relevant data and the techniques to be used in their analysis.

## Features /Characteristics of a Research Design

A good research design is flexible, appropriate, efficient, objective, reliable, valid, generalizable, and economical among others. A design which minimizes bias and maximizes the reliability of the data collected and analyzed is considered a good design. The design which gives the slightest experimental inaccuracy should be the best design in many studies. Similarly, a design which produces maximal evidence and offers a chance for considering many different aspects of a problem is considered most apt and efficient design in respect of many research problems. Therefore the question of a good design is associated to the purpose or objective of the research problem and also with the nature of the problem to be studied. A design may be quite suitable in one case, but may be found wanting in one respect or the other in the context of some other research problems. One single design cannot serve the purpose of all types of research problems. A research design appropriate for a particular research problem usually involves the following factors;

1. The means of obtaining information
2. The availability and skills of the researcher and his staff, if any
3. The objective of the problem to be studied
4. The nature of the problem to be studied and
5. The availability of time and money for the research work.

## Types of Research Design

There are many ways to classify research design but sometimes the distinction is artificial and other times different designs are combined. Nonetheless, a researcher needs to have a clear understanding of the various types of research designs to enable him/her select which type of research design to implement a study. These various research designs, all have their specific advantages and disadvantages. The one a researcher decides to use depends on the aims of the study and the nature of the phenomenon under study. Below offers a number of useful distinction between possible research designs.

1. Descriptive(example;- case study, naturalistic observation, survey)
2. Correlational (example;- case-control study, observational study)
3. Semi- experimental (example; - Field experiment, quasi-experiment)
4. Experimental ( Experiment with random assignment)
5. Review (example;- Literature review, Systematic review)
6. Meta-analytic(example;-Meta-analysis, i.e. using statistical methods for contrasting and combining results from different studies to identify patterns among study results, sources of disagreement among those results or other interesting relationship that may come to light in the context of multiple studies).

Research design can be classified broadly into ***quantitative*** and ***qualitative*** researched design.

## i. Qualitative Research Design

Qualitative research design is adopted when looking for more depth of a study. Qualitative research is multi-method in focused, involving an interpretive, naturalistic approach to its subject matter. This means that qualitative research design study things in their natural settings attempting to make sense of, or interpret phenomena in terms of the meanings people bring to them. Qualitative research design involves the studied use and collection of a variety of empirical materials (case study, personal experience, introspective, life story, interview, observational, and visual texts) –that describe routine problematic moments and meanings in individuals' lives. (Denzin and Lincoln, 2005:5 in Akerstrom, 2013). Researchers rely on qualitative research design where they are expected to conclude "why" a particular theory exists along with "what" respondents have to say about it. The aim of qualitative research is to understand the social reality of individuals, groups and culture as nearly as possible as its participants feel it or live it. Thus, people and groups, are studied in their natural setting.

### Advantages

1. Researcher gains an insider's view of the field because of his close involvement. This allows the researcher to find issues that are often missed (Such as subtleties and complexities) by the scientific, more positive inquiries.
2. Qualitative descriptions can play the important role of suggesting possible relationships, causes, effects and dynamic processes.
3. Qualitative research uses a descriptive, narrative style; this research might be of particular benefit to the practitioner as he or she could turn to qualitative reports in order to examine forms of knowledge that might otherwise be unavailable, thereby gaining new insight.
4. It can provide insights that are specific to an organization. The insight gained can lead to change of altitude, and add value to products/ services being offered, or look for ways to fix a declining reputation.
5. Creativity is the driving force. Qualitative research open ended question format of data collection for instance, allows the respondent to answer questions in their own way as they do not

need to answer questions in a way that pleases the researcher. Respondents are encouraged to be themselves. Consequently data collected can tend to have more accuracy.

6. It is flexible. The structure is not rigid. It only seeks authentic data and emotional responses. This generates more depth and complexities to the data collected. The qualitative research can thus follow any thought tangent and mine data from the answered provided.

## Disadvantages

1. With regard to the time and costs involved, qualitative designs do not generally draw samples from large –scale data sets.
2. The challenge of acceptable validity or reliability is a major criticism. Due to the subjective nature of qualitative data and its origin in single contexts, it is difficult to apply conformist standards of reliability and validity. For example, because of the central role played by the researcher in the generalization of data, it is not possible to replicate qualitative studies. Also, contexts, situations, events conditions, and interactions cannot be replicated to any extent nor can generalizations be made to a wider context than the one studied with any confidence.
3. The time required for data collection, analysis and interpretation are lengthy. Analysis of qualitative data is difficult and expert knowledge of an area is necessary to try to interpret qualitative data, and great care must be taken when doing so, for example, if looking for symptoms of mental illness.
4. It is not a statistically representative form of data collection- Qualitative research only provides data from perceptions which cannot be measured statistically. Only comparisons are possible, and that tends to create data duplication over time. If statistical data is required then qualitative research is not the form of design that should be utilized.
5. It relies upon the experience of the researcher- The data collected through qualitative research design is dependent upon the experience of the researchers involved in the process. Organization special data must be collected by a researcher that is familiar with the organization. Researchers must also have good interviewing skills, have the courage to ask follow up questions, and be able to form professional bonds with participants to ensure the accuracy of the data.

6. It may require multiple session- A Small sample size of research can be problematic. To make an important decision, numerous perceptions are often required to avoid making a costly mistake. This might mean having a multiple research sessions. This will mean a larger follow-up sample which conversely will create more costs
7. It can be difficult to replicate results-Qualitative research is based on individual or groups. This makes it almost impossible to duplicate the results that are found. Even the same person may have a different perception the next day than they had today. This makes qualitative research data collected through qualitative research difficult to verify, which can lead some to question the conclusions that researchers generate through this process.

## ii. Quantitative Research Design

Quantitative research design is based on numbers and statistics. Quantitative research design gathers data in a numerical form which can be put into categories, or in rank order, or measured in units of measurement. This type of data can be used to construct graphs and tables or raw data. It can be counted, or quantified. Thus, the quantitative research design is representative and implemented in cases where it is important for a researcher to have statistical conclusions to collect actionable insights. Numbers provide a better perspective to make important business/service delivery decisions. Quantitative research is important for the growth of any organization because any conclusion drawn on the basis of numbers and analysis will only prove to be effective for the organization. Quantitative research design aim to establish general laws of behavior and phenomenon across different settings/ contexts. Research is used to test a theory and ultimately support or reject it.

### Advantages of Quantitative Research

1. Quantitative research allows for a large sample size for any hypothesis. This makes it easier to reach an accurate generalization and makes the conclusion more credible.
2. With quantitative research collection data/ information is quick to gather. Experiments, surveys, and interviews provide immediate answers that become useful from a data-centered

approach. Fewer delays in the acquisition of these resources makes it easier to find correlations that eventually lead towards a useful conclusion.

3. This approach uses randomized process to collect information. This eliminates bias from appearing in most situations.
4. It validates itself since the results can easily be replicated; as quantitative research design focus on facts on a series of information.
5. Researchers can use the quantitative approach to focus on a specific fact that they want to study in the general population. Since the approach involves the use of numbers and statistics, the process allows a clear understanding of the reasons behind decisions, behaviours or actions from a group perspective.
6. It is statistically representative.

## Disadvantages of Quantitative Research

1. Quantitative research cannot be used to uncover in-depth knowledge of a phenomenon. For instance the process cannot be used to measure the ways in which a demographic segment or a group or society changes or how people interpret their actions or that of others.
2. It could be costly since it involves large number of sample size. If the cost is an issue, then quantitative research has a relevant barrier to ruminate. A situation where a single result may cost as much as #50,000, when a researcher is seeking for more data to analyze, may thwart the effort of the researcher.
3. Quantitative research sometimes creates unnatural environments.
4. Validity cannot easily be ascertained. The issue of validity always creates a cloud of doubt on the final results since there is no significant way to determine whether answers someone gives during a quantitative research effort are accurate. The process assumes that everyone is honest in every situation. Nonetheless, since observation is not always possible with quantitative research, the data always has a tinge of doubt to it, even when generalizing the results to the rest of the population.
5. The statistics gathered from quantitative research cannot produce specific feedback incidents that allow for positive refinement. (Green Garage, 2020).

Research design can further be considered under the following types among others:

## iii. Descriptive research design

In a descriptive research design, a researcher is solely interested in describing the condition or item under his/her research study. It is a theory-based research design which is created by gathering, analyzing and presenting collected data. By implementing an in-depth research design, a researcher can provide insights into the way and how of research. In other words, descriptive **research design helps provide answers to the questions of "who," "what," "when," "where" and "how"** associated with a particular research problem. With a descriptive research, the researcher will ascertain the characteristics of relevant demographic segment or groups without focusing on the "why" a certain phenomenon occurs. In other words it describes the subject of the research such as age, sex, occupation, income or education without covering the "why" it happens. Descriptive studies are normally factual and simple. However, such studies can be complex, demanding scientific skills on the part of researchers.

Descriptive studies are well structured. It tends to be rigid, and its approach cannot be changed often and again. In descriptive studies, the researcher has to give adequate thought to framing research questions and deciding the data to be collected and the procedure to be used for the purpose. Data collected may prove to be inadequate if the researcher is not careful in initial stages of data collection. Descriptive research designs are used for some definite purposes. Descriptive research cannot identify cause and effect relationship. Descriptive research can be conducted by using specific methods like observational method, case study method and survey methods (These will further be discussed later in this chapter).

Descriptive research can further be sub-divided into cross-sectional and longitudinal studies.

### a. Cross-sectional studies

Cross sectional study is a study involving a sample of elements from the population of interest at a single point in time. Such sample may deal with households, suppliers, students and other entities.

Information/data on a number of characteristics are collected from the sample elements. Such data are analyzed for drawing conclusions. Cross-sectional studies include field studies and surveys.

Field studies are conducted in real life situations such as schools, factories, institutions, etc. here, the inter relations among variables are studied under real setting. The cross-sectional analysis involves counting the simultaneous occurrence of the variables of interest. Field studies have certain merits and demerits. The important merit is that such studies are close to real life settings and cannot be criticized on the ground that they are away from real settings or are artificial. Field studies are also publicly important. However, such studies are scientifically inferior to laboratory and field experiments. There is also lack of precision in the measurement of variables. Cross-sectional research design studies are possible through survey. Survey research is wide in scope. Detailed information can be collected from a sample of a large population.

This method is also economical as more information can be collected per unit of cost. The time required for sample survey is also less than a census-inquiry. However in survey research more importance is given to information collection and not to be in-depth analysis. Secondly, survey research needs more time and money when conducted on a large scale. These studies can usually be conducted relatively faster and are expensive. The investigator measures outcome and the exposures in the study. Cross Sectional research designs have three distinctive features: no time dimension; a reliance on existing differences rather than change following intervention; and groups are selected based on existing differences rather than random allocation. The cross sectional design can only measure differences between or from among a variety of people, subjects, or phenomena rather than a process of change. As such, researchers using this design can only employ a relatively passive approach to making causal inferences based on findings.

## Benefits

1. Cross sectional studies provide a clear 'snapshot' of the outcome and the characteristics associated with it, at a specific point in time. Entails collection of data at one point in time,

cross sectional research is focused on finding relationships between variables at one moment in time.
2. Cross sectional designs focus on studying and drawing inferences between people, subjects, or phenomena.
3. Cross sectional studies are capable of using data from a large number of subjects and, is not geographically bound.
4. Can estimate prevalence of an outcome of interest because the sample is usually from the whole population.

### Hindrances

1. Results are static and time bound and, therefore, gives no indication of a sequence of events or reveal historical or temporal contexts.
2. Studies cannot be utilized to establish cause and effect relationships.
3. This design only provide a snapshot of analysis so there is always the possibility that a study could have differing results- if another time-frame had been chosen.
4. There is no follow up to the findings.

### b. Longitudinal studies

Longitudinal study is an observational research method in which data is gathered for the same subjects repeatedly over a period of time. It can extend over a short period, years or even decades. In a longitudinal study the same individuals/people are observed over the study period. In a longitudinal cohort for instance the same individuals are observed over the study, (that is longitudinal data). Longitudinal studies allow social scientist to distinguish short from long- term phenomena, such as poverty in a given society. It studies rapid fluctuations in behavior or thoughts, any emotions, from moment to moment or day to day in developmental psychology, to study developmental trends across the life span. Longitudinal studies can be cohort longitudinal. However, it is not all longitudinal studies that are cohort studies as longitudinal studies can instead include a group of people who do not share a common event. There are three types of longitudinal studies: *cohort longitudinal studies* samples a cohort/ a group of people who share a defining characteristics, typically they experienced a common event in a selected period such as birth or graduation) and perform cross section observations at intervals through time, nonetheless not all longitudinal research are cohort studies, as longitudinal studies can instead include a group of people who do not share a common event. *Panel Longitudinal* research design is another type of longitudinal studies. This is the *panel longitudinal study.* A panel is a sample of respondents who are interviewed not only once but thereafter from time to time. Here data to be collected relate to same variable but the measurements are taken repeatedly. There are many advantages and disadvantages of panel data. Panel data are suitable when the researcher undertakes detailed analysis. Similarly panel data are more comprehensive as compared to data collected from individual families. Finally, panel data collected is more accurate as compared to data collected through survey. These advantages of panel data improves the quality of research findings and conclusions. The limitations include that the panel used for collection may not be representative samples among others. The third is *the record linkage studies*. This type of longitudinal study, can be conducted without personal interviews by linking administrative records (for example, benefit receipts or census records) for the same individual over time. The advantage of using this type of longitudinal data are the potentially enormous sample sizes, which mean detailed analysis can be constructed for whole populations; by not having to conduct interviews, there is less risk of respondents dropout of reporting errors. These studies may be either prospective or retrospective in nature. However, the scope for using these types of study is limited by the nature of the records they are based on, which is unlikely to cover the range of areas of interest to researchers. It may also be difficult or impossible to use record linkage data because of concerns about confidentiality or privacy restrictions (Economic and Social Research Council (2020). Generally longitudinal studies do not require large number of participants.

## Advantages of Descriptive Research

1. Data collection: - Descriptive research can be conducted by using specific methods like observational method, case study method, and survey. Between these three all major methods of data collection provides a lot of information. This can be used for future research or even developing hypothesis of your research object.

2. Varied: - The opportunity to integrate the qualitative and quantitative methods of data collection gives the study a holistic understanding of a research topic. This cause data that was not planned to be collected, gets tracked and the data is varied, diverse and thorough.
3. Natural environment: - Descriptive research allows for the research to be conducted in the natural environment of the respondent and this ensures that high quality and honest data is collected.
4. Quick and Cheap: Descriptive research is less time consuming than quantitative experimental studies. As the sample size is generally large in descriptive research, the data collection is quick and cheap to conduct, than when data is collected on individual basis.
5. Basis for decision making;-Data collected from descriptive studies represents a larger population and is robust, it is easy to make decisions on the basis of the statistical analysis of that data. It is also effective to analyze non- quantified topics and issues.

## Disadvantages of Descriptive Research.

1. Sample is not representative: -The randomness of sample makes it very hard to accurately authenticate the sample as being a representation of the whole population. Moreover, descriptive studies cannot test or verify the research problem statistically.
2. Confidentiality:-Research results may reflect certain level of bias due to the absence of statistical tests. This can occur if questions are too personal and respondents feel they are being watched, they may therefore not be truthful in providing the answers required and this may affect the validity of the data.
3. The majority of descriptive studies are not "repeatable" due to their observational nature
4. No Scope to learn cause:-Descriptive studies are not helpful in identifying cause behind described phenomenon because descriptive studies only focuses on the what of an objective or phenomenon, it does not delve into the why or how and that is a limitation in understanding specific causes.

## iv. Experimental research design

Experimental research design is a classical scientific experiment. It is the most familiar design for individuals in physical sciences and many other fields of study. It is a scientific approach to research where one or more independent variables are manipulated and applied to one or more dependent variables to measure their effect on the latter. It is a casual research design where the effect caused by the independent variable on the dependent variable is observed. In this situation the researcher attempts to determine or predict what may occur. Experimental Research design is used to establish a relationship between the cause and effect of a situation. It is also referred to as causal research. Causal research design attempts to specify the nature of functional relationship between two or more variables. Experimental design makes predictions and conclusions on a subject matter. Data for casual research can be collected through field survey with the help of a questionnaire or by conducting laboratory experiment/controlled experiments.

The experimental design contains dependent, independent and extraneous variables. The dependent variables are the variables being treated or manipulated and are sometimes called the subject of the research. The independent variables are the experimental treatment being exerted on the dependent variables. Extraneous variables, on the other hand are other factors affecting the experiment that may also contribute to the change. The effect of the independent variables on the dependent variables is usually observed and recorded over some time, to aid researchers in drawing conclusion regarding the relationship between these two variables types. In doing this, the independent variable is administered to the experimental group and not to the control group, and both groups are measured on the same dependent variable. True experiments must have control, randomization, and manipulation. It is a highly practical research design method as it contributes towards solving a problem at hand. The independent variables are manipulated to monitor the change it has on the dependent variable.

Experimental research is often used where there is time priority in a causal relationship (a cause will always lead to the same effect), and the magnitude of the correlation is great. For example, the effect of an independent variable such as price on a dependent variable such as customer satisfaction on brand loyalty is monitored. This is conducted with a scientific approach using two sets of variables. The first set acts as a constant, which you use to measure the differences of the second set. Experimental research is mostly related to a laboratory test procedure; it research design involve collecting quantitative data and performing statistical analysis on them during research. It is often used in social sciences to observe human[41] behavior by analyzing two groups-effect of one group on the other. Experiments typically yield quantitative data, as they are concerned with measuring things, therefore, making it an example of quantitative research method. However, other research methods such as controlled observations and questionnaires can both produce quantitative information. Experimental study should establish a notable cause and effect. Experimental research gathers the data necessary to help the researcher make better decisions. Any research conducted under scientifically accepted conditions uses experimental methods. The success of experimental studies hinges on researches confirming the change of a variable is based solely on the manipulation of the constant variable. The research should establish a notable cause and effect relationship.

There are 3 basic types of experimental research design.

- Pre-experimental research design
- True experimental resign design and
- Quasi- experimental research design.

Pre-experimental research design: A group or various groups are kept under observation after implementing factors of cause and effect. You will conduct this research to understand whether further investigation is necessary for these particular groups. Pre-Experimental design is further subdivided into one- shot case study research Design, one-group pretest-posttest research design and static –group comparison.

True-experimental research design: It relies on statistical analysis to prove or disprove a hypothesis, making it the most accurate form of research design. Of the types of experimental design, only true design can establish a cause-effect relationship within a group. In a true experiment, three factors need to be satisfied via;

- A control group, which would not be subject to changes, and an Experimental group which will experience the changed variables.
- A variable which can be manipulated by the researcher
- Random distribution.

Quasi-experimental research design: The word "Quasi" indicates partial, half, pseudo or similarity. Therefore a Quasi-experimental research design is similar to the true experimental research, but it is not the same. In quasi-experimental the participants are not randomly assigned, and as such, they are used in settings where randomization is difficult or impossible. The difference between the two is the assignment of a control group. In this research, an independent variable is manipulated, but the participants of a group are not randomly assigned. Quasi-research is used in field settings where random assignment is either irrelevant or not required.

**Advantages:**

1. Experimental research makes an ideal starting point. The data you collect is a foundation on which to build more ideas and conduct research.
2. Experimental research design allows researchers to test their idea in a controlled environment and permits them to identify cause and effect relationships between variables and to distinguish placebo effects from treatment effects.
3. Approach provides the highest level of evidence for single studies and it is also useful for testing and validating already constructed theories.
4. Researchers have a stronger hold over variables to obtain desired results.
5. Results are specific.
6. Experimental research designs supports the ability to limit alternative explanations and to infer direct causal relationships in the study. Researchers can further analyze this relationship to determine more in-depth ideas to the extent that, it allows researchers to answer the question of "what causes something to occur."
7. After analyzing the results you can apply your findings to similar ideas or situations.

## Disadvantages

1. It is highly prone to human error due to its dependency on variable control which may not be properly implemented. Human responses in experimental research can be difficult to measure. Differently put, the artificial settings of experiments may alter the behaviours or responses of participants. These errors could eliminate the validity of the experiment and the research being conducted.
2. Exerting control of the extraneous variables may create unrealistic situations. Eliminating real life variables will result in researchers controlling the variables to suit his or her personal preferences.
3. It is a time –consuming process. So much time is spent on testing dependent variables and waiting for the effect of the manipulation of dependent variables to manifest.
4. It may be expensive- Experimental designs can be costly if special equipment of facilities are needed.
5. It is very risky and may have ethical complications that cannot be ignored. This is common in medical research, where failed trials may lead to a patient death or a deteriorating health condition.
6. Experimental research design results are not descriptive.
7. Response bias can also be supplied by the subject of the conversation.

## v. Correlational research design

Correlational research design attempts to determine the extent of a relationship between two or more variables using statistical data. Two different groups are required to conduct this research design method. There is no assumption while evaluating a relationship between two different variables and statistical analysis technique are used to calculate the relationship between them. Correlation between two variables is concluded using a correlation coefficient, whose value ranges between -1 and +1. If the correlation coefficient is towards +1, it indicates a positive relationship between the variables and -1 indicates a negative relationship between the two variables. In this type of research design relationship between and among a number of facts are sought and interpreted. Correlation research recognizes trends and patterns in data, but it does not go so far in its analysis to prove causes for these observed patterns, because cause and effect is not the basis of the design. The data relationships, and distributions of variables are studied only. Variables are not manipulated, they are only identified and are studied as they occur in a natural setting. Sometimes correlational research are considered as descriptive research, and not as its own type of research, as no variables are manipulated in the study.

Examples of correlational research design;

1. The relationship between intelligence and self-esteem
2. The relationship between diet and anxiety
3. The relationship between an aptitude test and success in an Arithmetic course
4. The relationship between the types of activities used in policy implementation and local government achievements
5. The relationship between smoking and lung diseases

## vi. Exploratory Research design

Exploratory research design is the most commonly unstructured, and informal research. It is the preliminary research that clarifies the exact nature of the problem to be solved. It is undertaken to gain background information about the general nature of the research problem (Alvin and Roland, 2003). The central purpose of exploratory research is to know the unknown. This also narrows the scope of the research. To explore means to find out causes/ reasons behind a specific problem with the aim of formulating hypotheses regarding potential problems and opportunities present in the decision situation. It is the starting point in all types of research project. It helps to define the problem precisely.

In exploratory research design, the researcher's ideas and thoughts are key as it is primarily dependent on their personal inclination about a particular topic. Explanation about unexplored aspects of a subject is provided along with details about what, how and why related to the research questions. It can further be said that an exploratory research design is conducted about a research problem when there are few or no earlier studies to refer to or rely upon to predict an outcome. The focus is on gaining insights and familiarity for later investigation or undertaken when research problems are in a preliminary stage of investigation. In

Leinhardt (1980) opinion, the hypothesis can be tested at a later phase with a conclusive research design. Exploratory designs are often used to establish an understanding of how best to proceed in studying an issue or what methodology would effectively apply to gathering information about the issue. The technique include secondary research such as reviewing available literature and/or data, informal qualitative approaches, such as discussions with members of the public, employees, management or competitors. Formal qualitative research (through in-depth interviews, focus groups, projective methods, case studies or pilot studies, can be adopted to achieve this type of research design. According to Malek and Massoud, (2011) for the objective of identification of problem, it can be assisted through three ways, which are: searching secondary sources, interviewing knowledgeable persons, and compiling case histories.

### Advantages of Exploratory research design

The goals of exploratory research are intended to produce the following possible insights:

1. Exploratory research design is useful for gaining background information on a particular topic, it thus provides an opportunity for the development of tentative theories and/or hypotheses; the determination of the feasibility of a study in the future are also made possible. In other words the direction for future research and techniques get developed.
2. It identifies relevant course of action and defines new terms and clarify existing concepts.
3. It defines the problem more specifically or precisely.
4. Exploratory research design establishes priorities for further research
5. It isolates key variables and relationships for further examination
6. Exploratory research design makes issues get refined for more systematic investigation and formulation of new research question and provides a well-grounded picture of the situation being developed.
7. Exploratory research is flexible and can address research questions of all types (what, why, how).

8. In the policy arena or applied to practice, exploratory studies help establish research priorities and where resources should be allocated.

### Disadvantages

1. Exploratory research generally utilizes small sample sizes and thus, findings are typically not generalizable to the population at large.
2. The exploratory nature of the research inhibits an ability to make definitive conclusions about the findings. They provide insight but not definitive conclusions.
3. The research process underpinning exploratory studies is flexible but often unstructured, leading to only tentative results that have limited value to decision- makers.
4. Design lacks rigorous standards applied to methods of data gathering and analysis because one of the areas for exploration could be to determine what method or methodologies could best fit the research problem, etc.

## Some other research designs include;

### a. Case Study Research Design

The case study research design have evolved over the past few years as a useful tool for investigating trends and specific situations in many academic disciplines. This design is commonly used in the social sciences. It is a research strategy, usually empirical inquiry that investigates a phenomenon within its context. It is descriptive and exploratory. The observations of a phenomenon may be very valuable, with reference to a certain community or a certain culture. It is often used to narrow down a very broad field of research into one or a few easily researchable topics. The case study research design is also useful for testing whether a specific theory and model actually applies to phenomena in the real world. They are important ways of illustrating theories and can help show how different aspects of a person's life are related to each other. It is a useful design when not much is known about a phenomenon. They help to generate new ideas, and systems that are studied holistically by one or more methods. A case study is based on opinion unlike a scientific design study which is based on facts. Here is an example of a case study in social science: *"Critically analyze the Challenges and Prospects of*

*Housing Policy in Nigeria: A case study of Oredo Local Government Area.*" A case study in social science is usually a detailed analysis of a person or group especially as a model of medical, psychiatric, psychological, or social phenomena and a detailed intensive study of a unit, such as a corporation or a division,that stresses factors contributing to its success or failure. The act or an instance of analyzing one or more particular case or cases histories with a view to making generalizations. A detailed analysis of a person or group from a social or psychological or medical point of view. Analysis involves an investigation of the component parts of a whole and their relations in making up the whole

## Types of Case Study:

Under the more generalized category of case study exists several subdivisions, each of which is custom selected for use depending upon the goals and/or objective of the investigator. They include the following:

1. Illustrative case Studies: These are primarily descriptive and designed to shed light on a particular situation, set of circumstances, and the social relations and processes that are embedded in them. They typically utilize one or two instances of an event to show what a situation is like. Illustrative case studies serve primarily to make the unfamiliar familiar and to give readers a common language about the topic in question.
2. Exploratory (Pilot) Case Studies: These are condensed case studies performed before implementing a large scale investigation. Their basic function is to help identify questions and select types of measurement prior to the main investigation. The primary snag of this type of study is that initial findings may seem convincing enough to be released prematurely as conclusions.
3. Cumulative Case Studies: These serve to aggregate information from several sites collected at different times. The idea behind these studies is that collection of past studies will allow for greater generalization without additional cost or time being expanded on new, possibly repetitive studies.
4. Critical Instance Case Studies: These examine one or more sites for either the purpose of examining a situation of unique interest with little to no interest in generalizability, or to call into question or challenge a highly generalized or universal

assertion. This method is useful for answering case and effect questions. ( https://writing.colostate.edu)

## Advantages

1. Some argue that because a case study is such a narrow field its results cannot be extrapolated to fit an entire question and that they show only one narrow example. On the other hand, it is argued that a case study provides more realistic responses than a purely statistic responses than a purely statistical survey.
2. It is believed that a case study design is advantageous as it can focus on specific and interesting cases. This may be an attempt to test a theory with a typical case or it can be a specific topic that is of interest.
3. Approach excels at bringing us to an understanding of a complex issue through detailed contextual analysis of a limited number of events are conditions and their relationships.
4. A researcher using the case study research design can apply a variety of methodologies and rely on a variety of sources to investigate a research problem.
5. Design can extend experience or add strength to what is already known through previous research.
6. Social scientists, in particular, make wide use of this research design to examine contemporary real-life situations and provide the basis for application of concepts and theories and extension of methods.
7. The design can provide detailed descriptions and specific and rare cases.

## Disadvantages.

1. Single or small number of cases offers little basis for establishing reliability or to generalize the findings to a wider population of people, places, or things.
2. The intense exposure to study of the case may bias a researcher's interpretation of the findings.
3. Design does not facilitate assessment of cause and effect relationships
4. Vital information may be missing, making the case hard to interpret.
5. The case may not be representative or typical of the larger problem being investigated.

6. If the criteria for selecting a case is because it represents a very unusual or unique phenomenon or problem for study, then your interpretation of the findings can only apply to that particular case.

*NOTE: This Case Study section benefitted immensely from the works of State University Case Study writing guides.*

## b. Observational Design

The term observational research design refers to several different types on non-experimental studies in which behaviour is systematically observed and recorded. It is a non-experimental design because nothing is manipulated or controlled so non causal conclusions using this approach is arrived at. It involves the researcher using all of his senses to examine people in natural settings or naturally occurring situations. Observation of a field setting involves prolonged engagement in a setting of social situation. There are two general types of observational designs. In direct observations, people know that you are watching them. Unobtrusive measures involve any method for studying behavior where individuals do not know they are being observed. An observational study allows a useful insight into a phenomenon and avoids the ethical and practical difficulties of setting up a large and cumbersome research project. It is aimed to describe a variable or set of variables. The data collected under these studies are often qualitative in nature but may be quantitative also or both (mixed methods).

### Advantages

1. Observational studies are usually flexible and do not necessarily need to be structured around a hypothesis about what you expect to observe (data is emergent rather than pre-existing).
2. The researcher is able to collect in-depth information about a particular behavior.
3. It can reveal interrelationships among multifaceted dimensions of group interactions.
4. You can generalize your results to real life situations.
5. Observational research design is useful for discovering what variables may be important before applying other methods like experiments.

6. Observation research designs account for the complexity of group behaviors

### Disadvantages

Reliability of data is low because seeing behaviors occur over and over again may be a time consuming task and are difficult to replicate.

1. In observational research, findings may only reflect a unique sample population and, thus, cannot be generalized to other groups.
2. There can be problem with bias as the researchers may only "see what they want to see."
3. There is no possibility to determine "cause and effect" relationships since nothing is manipulated.
4. Sources or subjects may not all be equally credible.
5. Any group that is knowingly studied is altered to some degree by the presence of the researcher, therefore, potentially skewing any data collected.

### c. Philosophical Design

Understood more as an abroad approach to examining a research problem than a methodological design, philosophical analysis and argumentation is intended to challenge deeply embedded, often intractable, assumptions underpinning an area of study. This approach uses the tools of argumentation derived from philosophical traditions, concepts, models, and theories to critically explore and challenge, for example, the relevance of logic and evidence in academic debates, to analyze arguments about fundamental issues, or to discuss the root of existing discourse about a research problem. These overarching tools of analysis can be framed in three ways:

1. Ontology- the study that describes the nature of reality; for example, what is real and what is not, what is fundamental and what is derivative?
2. Epistemology- the study that explores the nature of knowledge; for example, on what does knowledge, for example, on what does knowledge and understanding depend upon and how can be certain of what we know?
3. Axiology- the study of values; for example, what values does an individual or group hold and why? How are values related to

interest, desire, will, experience, and difference between a matter of fact and a matter of value?

## Advantages

1. Can provides a basis for applying ethical decision-making to practice.
2. Functions as a means of gaining greater self-understanding and self- knowledge about the purposes of research.
3. Brings clarity to general guiding practices and principles of an individual or group.
4. Philosophy informs methodology.
5. Refine concepts and theories that are invoked in relatively unreflective modes of thoughts and discourse.
6. Beyond methodology, philosophy also informs critical thinking about epistemology and the structure of reality (metaphysics).
7. Offers clarity and definition to the practical and theoretical uses of terms, concepts, and ideas.

## Disadvantages

1. Limited application to specific research problems (answering the so what question in social science research).
2. Analysis can be abstract, argumentative, and limited in its practical application to real-life issues.
3. While a philosophical analysis may render problematic that was once simple or taken for Granted, the writing can be dense and subject to unnecessary jargon, overstatement, and/or excessive quotation and documentation.
4. There are limitation in the use of metaphor as a vehicle of philosophical analysis.
5. There can be analytical difficulties in moving from philosophy to advocacy and between abstract through and application to the phenomenal world.

## d. Survey research design

The survey research design is commonly used in social sciences since the researcher has no control over the dependent and dependent variables. A survey research refers to a process of eliciting data from a target population through either questionnaire or interview instrument, and subjecting such data to statistical analysis for the purpose of drawing conclusions (Obasi, 1999). Through questionnaires and interviews, survey research: Makes it possible to measure what a person knows (knowledge or information), what a person likes and dislikes (values and preferences), and what a person thinks (attitudes and beliefs). Questionnaires and interviews can also be used to discover what experiences have taken place (biography) and what is occurring at the present. This information can be transformed into numbers or quantitative data by using the attitude scaling or by counting the number of respondents who give a particular response thus generating frequency data (Tuckman, 1972:173). The above point of view suggests that the purpose of research design is to ascertain whether quantitative data will validate or invalidate existing perceptions and belief about a given phenomenon through critical analysis of results obtained from field survey. Moreover, Tafida (2005) observed that "the major characteristic of all survey designs is a lack of control." He went further to say that "the investigator is concerned with observing what is happening to sample subject/variables without any attempt to manipulate or control them."

### e. Historical Design

According to Ujo (1999), historical research design is a systematic and objective inquiry into events, development and experiences of the past. Historical research differs from other forms of research in the sense that it is always concerned with the past and calls for a more difficult type of data interpretation. The purpose of a historic design is to collect, verify, and synthesize evidence from the past to establish facts that defend or refute a hypothesis. It uses secondary sources which comprise accounts of events by persons who did not directly observe the event. Information from books or newspapers and archival records in form of diaries, tapes, antiques, photographs, audio and visual recordings drawings and painting are used as secondary sources. Whenever primary sources are available, in form of direct information as accounts of eyewitness and historical objects which can be directly examined or measured, to use secondary sources would be considered as serious error for the obvious reason that secondary sources are usually very susceptible to distortions and hence may not be authentic as the primary sources. The limitation is that the sources must be both authentic and valid. In evaluating the data collected, two forms of criticisms; external and internal are employed (Ujo, 2004).

## Characteristics

- Historical design involves the careful study and analysis of data about past events.
- It is critical investigation of events , their development, experiences of past
- The purpose is to gain clearer understanding of the important of past on present and future events related to life processes
- Involves the review of written materials but may include oral documentation as well.
- Typically relies on available data which are in form of dairies, letters, newspaper, reports and so on.
- It covers categories such as historical legal documentary, bibliographical, biographical, institutional and organizational.

## Areas of Historic Study

1. Periods:- Historic study focus on events and developments that occurred during particular blocks of time names in order to allow the organization of ideas and classificatory generalization to be used by these researchers.
2. Geographical Location: particular geographical locations can form the basis of historical study. Example: continents, countries and cities.
3. Military History: concentrates on the study of conflicts that have happened in human society. This includes examining the wars, battles, military strategies, and weaponry.

## Methods and tools used in Historical Research

1. Contemporaneous corroboration:
2. Photography: A methodological tool for collection of all known information about individuals in a given period.it is further support provided by the existing evidence about the past events. It is powerful method used to establish facts beyond their furnished limited lifespans.
3. Historical revisionism: traditionally used in completely natural sense to describe the work or idea of historian who has revised a previously accepted view of a particular topic.
4. Change log: log or record of changes made to a project such as website or software project.

5. Human evolution: process of change and development or evolution by which human beings emerged as distinctively special.
6. Social Change: Changes in nature, social institutions, social behavior or the social relations of a society or community of people.

### Advantages

1. The historic research design is unobtrusive: then act of research does not affect the results of the study.
2. The historic approach is well suited for trend analysis.to more fully understand and interpret
3. Historical records can add important contextual background required to more fully understand and interpret a research problem.
4. There is often no possibility of researcher subject interaction that could affect the findings.
5. Historic sources can be used over and over to study different research problems or to replicate a previous study.

### Disadvantages

1. The ability to fulfill the aims of your research are directly related to the amount and quality of documentation available to understand the research problem.
2. Since historic research relies on data from the past, there is no way to manipulate it to control for contemporary contexts.
3. Interpreting historic sources can be very time consuming.
4. The sources of historical materials must be archived consistently to ensure access. This may especially be challenging for digital or online–only sources.
5. Original authors bring their own perspectives and these biases are more difficult to ascertain in historical resources.
6. Due to lack of control over external variables, historical research design is very weak with regard to internal validity.
7. It is rare that the entirety of historical documentation needed to fully add a research problem is available for interpretation, therefore, gaps need to be acknowledged.

### f. Sequential Research Design

Sequential research is carried out in a deliberate, staged approach (i.e. serially) where one stage will be completed, followed by another, then another, and so on, with the aim that each will build upon the previous one until enough data is gathered over an interval of time to test your hypothesis. The sample size is not predetermined. After each sample is analyzed, the researcher can accept the null hypothesis, accept the alternative hypothesis, or select another pool of subjects and conduct the study once again. This means the researcher can obtain a limitless number of subjects before making a decision whether to accept the null or alternative hypothesis. Using a quantitative framework, a sequential study generally utilizes sampling techniques to gather data and applying statistical methods to analyze the data. Using a qualitative framework, sequential studies generally utilize samples of individuals or groups of individuals or (cohorts) and use qualitative methods, such as interviews or observations, to gather information from each sample.,

### Advantages

1. The researcher has a limitless option when it comes to sample size and the sampling schedule.
2. Due to the repetitive nature of this research design, minor changes and adjustments can be done during the initial parts of the research method. Useful design for exploratory studies.
3. There is very effort on the part of the researcher when performing this technique. It is generally not expensive, time consuming, or workforce extensive.
4. Because the study is conducted serially the study is conducted serially, the results of one sample are known before the next sample is taken and analyzed.

### Disadvantages

1. Retrieved approaching representativeness is when the researcher chooses to use a very large sample size significant enough to represent a significant portion of the entire population. In this case, moving on to study a second or more sample can be difficult.
2. Because the sampling technique is not randomized, the design cannot be used to create conclusions and interpretations that pertain to an entire population. Generalizability from findings is limited.

3. Difficult to account for and interpret variation from one sample to another over time, particularly when using qualitative methods of data collection.

## References

Academia Stack Exchange (2016) "What is the difference between a Panel Study and a Cohort Study" @ https://academia.stackexchange.com retrieved 23/6/2020

Adekeye, J. A. (2016). "Empirical Application of Research Design in Management Sciences" *Net Journal of Business Management*, 4 (2) 15-21.

Akhtar, Md. Inaam. (2016). "Research Design" *Research in Social Science: Interdisciplinary Perspectives@https://www.ssrn.com retrieved 23/6/ 2020*

Anastas, Jeane W. (1999). *Research Design for social Work and the Human Services. Flexible Methods: Descriptive Research.* 2nd edition. New York Columbia University Press.

Anikpo, M. (1986). *Foundations of Social Science Research: A methodological Guide for Students:* Enugu, ABIC Publishers.

Bailey, Carol R and Carol A. Bailey. *A guide to Qualitative Field Research.* Thousand Oaks (2017). CA: Sage.

Black, T. R. (1999). *Doing quantitative research in the social sciences: An integrated approach to research design, measurement and statistics,* sage.

Burgess, Robert G. (2002). "Conducting Field Research." *An Introduction to field Research.* New York: Rutledge.

Carr, L.T. (1994). "The strengths and weaknesses of quantitative and qualitative research: what methods for nursing?" *Journal of advanced nursing,* 20(4), 716-721.

Creswell, J. W. & Creswell, J. D. (2018). *Research Design: Qualitative, Quantitative, and mixed Methods Approaches.* 5th edition. Published by Los Angeles: Sage @ https://cmc.marrmot.org retrieved 22/6/2020

Cooper, R. D. and Schindler, S. P. (2001). *Business Research Methods*, McGraw-Hill Irvin, 7th edition.

De Vaus, D. A. (2006) *Research Design in Social Research*, London: sage.

Denzin, Norman K, and Yvonna S. Lincoln, (2005). "Introduction. The Discipline and practice of qualitative research," in *The Sage handbook of qualitative research*, ed. Norman K. Denzin Curiosity and Serendipity in qualitative research. Qualitative Sociology Review 9 (2): 10-18.

Ethridge, D. E.(2004) *Research Methodology in Applied Economics*, John Wiley & sons, p.24

Fox, W. & Bayat, M.S. (2007) "A *Guide to Managing Research*" Juta Publications, p.45.

Green, Garage (2020) "15 Advantages and Disadvantages of quantitative Research" @ *https://greengarageblog.org accessed* on 15/6/2020

Healy P. Devanse D. "Methodological Considerations in Cohort Study Designs." Nurse Researcher 18 (2011): 32-36; Glenn, Norval D. editor, *Cohort Analysis*. 2nd edition.

Thousand Oaks, CA: Sage, 2005; Levin, Kate Ann. Study Design 1V: Cohort Studies.
http://www.essayforum.com/grammar-usage-13/to-write-366/
http://www..gttp.org/docs/HowToWriteAGo
htpp://writing.colostate.edu/guides/researchState University Case Study writing guides

Kerlinger, F. N. (1977). *Foundations of Behavioural Science*. Holt, Rinehart and Winston, Inc.

Laxmi Thapa (2017). "Historical Research Design" in Slide Share. https://www. slideshare net> mobile.

Leedy, P. D. (1997). *Practical Research Planning and Design.*6th edition. New Jersey: Prentice-Hill.

Leinhardt, Gaea, and Samuel Leinhart (1980). "Exploratory Data Analysis: New Tools for the Analysis of Empirical Data" *Review of Research in Education 8* (1980): 85-157.*http://www.jstor.org/stable*/10.2307/ 1167124

Lugtig, Peter, and Smith Paul. A. (2019). The Choice between a Panel and Cohort Study Design@ https://eprints.soton.ac.uk retrieved 29/6/2020

Martyn Shuttleworth (2008). "Case Study Research Design." Retrieved Jun, 09, 2020 from Explorable.com:https://explortable.com/case-study-research-design

McLeod, S. A. (2019, July 30).

Descombe, M. (2010). Qualitative vs. quantitative research. Simply Psychology, *in The Good research guide: for small-scale social research* McGraw-Hill in Https://www.simplypsychology.org/quaitative-quantitative,html

https://writing.colostate.edu Types of case studies Writing @ CSU Colorado State Universityaccessed 9/6/2020

Nnamdi, A. (1999). *Research Methodology in Behavioural Science*, Ibadan Longman Nigeria PLC

Norman K. Denzin and Yvonna S. Lincoln (1994). "Ethnography and Participant Observation," in *Handbook of Qualitative Research. Observational Research.* (ed.) Thousand Oaks, CA: Sage, Pp. 248-261;

Nwana, O. C. (1981). *Introduction to Education Research.* Ibadan, Heinemann Educational Books Ltd.

Obasi, I. N. (1999): *Research Methodology in Political Science*. Enugu: Academic Publishing Company.

Ogunbameru, O. A. (2000). *Introducing Social Research and Report Writing*. Ibadan: Pat-Mag Press.

Onwe, O. J. (1998). *Elements of Project and Dissertation Writing: A Guide to Effective Dissertation Report*, Lagos: Impressed Publishers.

Onwe, O. J. (2007). *Statistical Methods for Business and Economic Decisions: A Practical Approach*, Lagos, Samalice Press.

Osuala, E. C. (2001). *Introduction to Research Methodology* (3rd Edition). Onitsha: Africana-Feb. Publishers, Ltd.

Punch, K. (1998). *Introduction to social Research quantitative and qualitative Approaches,* London: Sage.

Susan White (2019) "AllAssignmentHelp" Academic Assignment Help issignmenthelp.com.accessed 7/6/2020.

Tafida, A. D. (2005). "Research Design / Research Methodology in the Social and Management Sciences." A *Publication of Public Administration Department*, University of Abuja. Abuja: Joyce Publishers.

Trochim, William, Donnelly James, P and Arora, Kanika (2015), *Research Mrthodology: The Essential Knowledge Base*, United Kingdom CENGAGE Learning.

Tuckman, B. W. (1972). *Conducting Educational Research.* New York: Harcourt Brace Jovanovich, Inc.

Ujo, A. A. (2004). *Understanding Social Research in Nigeria.* Kaduna: Joyce Graphic Printer and publishers.

UKRI (2020) "Economic and Social Research Council," Learning Hub learning.closer.ac.uk.record retrieved 0n 23/6/2020@https??

Wikipedia, (2009).*Cross sectional studies Design, Application, Strengths and Weaknesses of a cross- sectional Study, Studies.* Cross sectional, Health Knowledge.

Yvonna S. Lincoln, 1-32 Thousand Oaks: Sage Publications *https://link.springer. com>article* accessed on 15/06/2020

# CHAPTER FOUR
# LITERATURE REVIEW

## Harrison Eromosele

### Introduction

"The pursuit of man is the pursuit of knowledge" (Skolimowski, 1967). Man's continual quest for new and superior knowledge enables him to progress beyond his present frontiers of achievement and development. This is understandable as he is uniquely endowed with the capacity, which through the process of inquiry, enables him to gain more and clearer insight into the complex phenomena of nature and to understand his environment better. The act of inquiry had since the $16^{th}$ century, evolved into a scientific process called research. Interestingly, an effective research must be associated with a series of reviews of existing body of knowledge. This is an important step in the research process and has been identified as what we now understand to be the literature review. Indeed, a modern day research is incomplete without the component of literature review. This is because of the important role literature review plays in the course of carrying out a research. Literature review is the symbolic compass that informs the researcher of the current status of a subject matter in the existing body of knowledge and indicates the likely appropriate direction to follow in breaking new grounds in a manner that beneficially adds to the available body of knowledge. For one thing, past and present information about a research topic are important prerequisite to build upon, if clumsy and muddled ideas are to be avoided. "Therefore, the need to uncover what is already known in the body of knowledge prior to initiating any research study should not be underestimated" (Hart, 1998). This means that every relevant piece of information pertaining to an area of research interest is needed for further conceptual, theoretical and empirical advancement. Like Jankowiz puts it: *Knowledge doesn't exist in a vacuum and your work only has value in relation to other people. Your work and your findings will be significant only to the extent that they're the same as, or different from, other people's work and findings.*

This chapter is dedicated to explain in a simple and clear terms, the meaning, purpose, essential steps, characteristics, plagiarism, and types, of a literature review in terms their basic concepts and elements. Accordingly, the issues below are of specific interest for discussion:

1.2 Meaning of literature review
1.3 Purpose of literature review
1.4 Essential steps to follow in writing a literature review
1.5 Characteristics of a well written literature reviews
1.6 Plagiarism in literature review.
1.7 Types of literature review sources

## Meaning of Literature Review

Literature review is a process that is required of a researcher to understand the available past and present information relating to his area of research interest or topic on which he builds new and superior knowledge that better addresses existing realities and issues. Essentially, it summarizes and extracts in a synthetic, evaluative and interpretative manner the main information related to his research topic from a pool of available research studies. This meaning is somewhat generic as it may have left out some specific details, as can be seen from the following authors' below definitions:

A literature review is a surveys scholarly articles, books and other sources relevant to a particular issue, area of research, or theory, and by so doing, providing a description, summary, and critical evaluation of these works. Literature reviews are designed to provide an overview of sources you have explored while researching a particular topic and to demonstrate to your readers how your research fits into the larger field of study (libguides.usc.edu, n.d.).

A literature review is a description of the literature relevant to a particular field or topic. It gives an overview of what has been said, who the key writers are, what are the prevailing theories and hypotheses, what questions are being asked, and what methods and methodologies are appropriate and useful. As such, it is not in itself primary research, but rather it reports on other findings (Emerald Group Publishing, n.d.).

The selection of available documents (published and unpublished) on the topic, containing information, ideas, data and evidence written from a particular standpoint to fulfil certain aims or express certain views on the nature of the topic and how it is to be investigated, and the effective evaluation of these documents in relation to the research being proposed. (Hart. 2001, p 13).

The above definitions of literature review by the different authors suggest that it can be a source of solid foundation for the advancement of the body of knowledge. Important points are stated by the authors, yet, not all together exhaustive. However, one point we have decided to emphasize from the above is the fact that literature review is not the discovery of new knowledge but rather a summary of a thorough assessment of already available and accessible research works. More so, any who does not do a thorough review of related existing and accessible research material of his topic before delving fully into it may work risk the peril of committing duplication of effort and plagiarism. Indeed, the researcher uses the literature as a foundation and a support for a new insight that he contributes. The literature review however, is to summarize and synthesize the arguments and ideas of others with adding new contributions. (Ramdhan, A., Ramdhani, M. A., and Amin, A. S.(2014)). A summary is a recap of the important information of the source, but a synthesis is a re-organization, or a reshuffling, of that information. It might give a new interpretation of old material or combine new with old interpretations. Or it might trace the intellectual progression of the field, including major debates. And depending on the situation, the literature review may evaluate the sources and advise the reader on the most pertinent or relevant. (writingcenter.unc.edu). This means that the available research material should be critically examined rather than just summarizing it.

By critical examination of the research materials we mean to do a thorough study of the material under review so as to identify its information boundary, or scope, weakness and strength, gaps in the literature, and to enable the researcher to coordinate a host of related materials (i.e., to relate the information contained in one material to another), without downplaying on the uniqueness of each related material.

## Purpose of a Literature Review

The purpose of considering a literature review in research is diverse. We explain some major ones below:

1. To have a broad perspective of what other researches have done relating to the topic.
2. To enable the research to identify the effort duplication, inconsistency and gaps in the existing body of literature.
3. To be familiar with new terminologies (jargons) which aid the researcher to earn a mastery of the fundamentals (basics) in the research topic.
4. To enable the researchers the opportunity to compare and assess various related research materials which equips him better to carry out the research task.
5. To identify key conclusions and findings of related research materials.
6. To know from the start whether the research task is an assignment to embark upon.
7. To know the place of existing theories related to the research.
8. To enable the researcher to build his own unique method of the research.
9. To know what skills are required to carry out the task.
10. To identify what theory one can adopt or build upon to suit your own research task.
11. To identify one's research task in the specific field of the literature.

## Essential Steps to follow in writing a Literature Review

We briefly explain in simple and in clear terms the sequential steps to follow in carrying out a literature review. This pattern has a way of encouraging or stimulating interest particularly in novel researchers.

1. Read a textbook in your discipline or in your research area of interest. As you do that, prepare your mind to look out for topic(s). Select a researchable topic among your topics of interest, particularly the one you think you can handle best.

2. After the selection process of the researchable topic that most interest you, narrow your reading and perhaps questioning to specifics: chapters of textbooks; articles; conferences; open discussions essentially with mentors in the area and other scholars; corporate or government periodic reports that are related to the topic under consideration. In this phase, you may even be more equipped enough to modify or paraphrase the topic. Remember avoid too broad a topic. One way the researcher should be effective in the selection of source materials is to go for research materials with recent references.
3. Once the researcher has succeeded in selecting research materials, suitable for the research task, the next step is to look out for those materials that have research summary or abstract section. This is typically found at the beginning of the research materials (articles) or at the end of the research material (textbook). While there is still need to consider the content of the material, the summary or abstract section is an incentive for the researcher to peruse as many related materials as sufficiently possible. This process broadens his capacity to comprehend the terminologies related to the conceptual issues. It also enriches the researcher with enough information to colour his review. It enriches the researcher with the power to evaluate and synthesize the available articles and to develop the appropriate skill in establishing the relationship that will run through the literature review.
4. Organization: The literature review needs to be organized in a way that it establishes a flow from the introduction of the literature review to the body and thereafter to the conclusive section. This will enable the reader to easily understand and appreciate the work.

In table 1.1 below is a more comprehensive step by step writing of a literature review as documented by the University of the FRASER VALLEY

## Table 1.1

| **Nine Steps to Writing a Literature Review** |
|---|
| **1. Find a working topic.** |
| Look at your specific area of study. Think about what interests you, and what is fertile ground for study. Talk to your professor, brainstorm, and read lecture notes and recent issues of periodicals in the field. |

**2. Review the literature.**
Using key words, search a computer database. It is best to use at least two databases relevant to your discipline.
Remember that the reference lists of recent articles and reviews can lead to valuable papers.
Make certain that you also include any studies contrary to your point of view.
**3. Focus your topic narrowly and select papers accordingly.**
Consider the following:
What interests you? ii. What interests others? iii. What time span of research will you consider?
Choose an area of research that is due for a review.
**4. Read the selected articles thoroughly and evaluate them.**
What assumptions do most/some researchers seem to be making?
What methodologies do they use? - what testing procedures, subjects, material tested?
Evaluate and synthesize the research findings and conclusions drawn.
Note experts in the field: names/labs that are frequently referenced.
Note conflicting theories, results, methodologies.
Watch for popularity of theories and how this has/has not changed over time.
**5. Organize the selected papers by looking for patterns and by developing sub- topics.**
Note things such as:
i..Findings that are common/contested. ii. Two or three important trends in the research. iii.The most influential theories.
**6. Develop a working thesis.**
Write a one- or two-sentence statement summarizing the conclusion you have reached about the major trends and developments you see in the research that has been done on your subject.
**7. Organize your own paper based on the findings from steps 4 & 5.**
Develop headings/subheadings. If your literature review is extensive, find a large table surface, and on it place post-it notes or filing cards to organize all your findings into categories. Move them around if you decide that (a) they fit better under different headings, or (b) you need to establish new topic headings.
**8. Write the body of the paper.**
Follow the plan you have developed above, making certain that each section links logically to the one before and after, and that you have divided your sections by themes or subtopics, not by reporting the work of individual theorists or researchers.
**9. Look at what you have written; focus on analysis, not description.**
Look at the topic sentences of each paragraph. If you were to read only these sentences, would you find that your paper presented a clear position, logically developed, from beginning to end? If, for example, you find that each paragraph begins with a researcher's name, it might indicate that, instead of evaluating and comparing the research literature from an analytical point of

view, you have simply described what research has been done. This is one of the most common problems with student literature reviews. So if your paper still does not appear to be defined by a central, guiding concept, or if it does not critically analyse the literature selected, then you should make a new outline based on what you have said in each section and paragraph of the paper, and decide whether you need to add information, to delete off-topic information, or to re-structure the paper entirely.

Source: University of the Fraser Valley

## Characteristics of Well Written Literature Reviews

1. It must follow the outline presented in the content of the work
2. It should as much as possible be objective. This means that the researcher should present relevant facts that both support and do not support his analysis and position. This requires a display of moral instinct on the part of the writer.
3. The literature should focus only on materials that are related and relevant to the research question(s) and these alone should be cited.
4. The literature review must be organized. Indeed, it should be structured in a manner that exhibits flows and such that in the end it addresses or emphasizes the research question(s). An effective way of doing this is by sub-headings. For instance, a literature review may be sub-headed into the following: Introduction, conceptual literature, theoretical literature, empirical literature and gaps in the literature. We present a brief explanation for each.

**Introduction**: This informs the reader subjects (topics) and issues discussed.

**Conceptual literature**: Explaining key words or statements related to the work and how various authors have applied these words.

**Theoretical literature**: This identifies existing theories related to the work and examines how their links align with it. Theories should be linked up with another. It does not matter whether the theories conform or contrast each other.

**Empirical literature**: This demonstrates when, how and in what context existing theories are practically related to the work. It is a practical experiment or test conducted on the theories to authenticate their validity in relation to the research question(s).

**Gaps in the literature**: This examines issues of concerns relevant to the study or work but which lack clarifications. Also, it may be issues in the literature not adequately addressed.

One effective way of injecting a flow in the structure of a literature review is by using linked words like: correspondingly, similarly, besides, also etc. these words systematically link views that are in conformity. Others like: however, nonetheless, conversely, systematically link contrasting views. The act will enable the researcher to clearly show the possible relationships that may exist among the different research materials used in the study.

## Types of literature Review sources

The researcher can sort information from a host of sources some of which are : Journal articles like surveys, and research papers that are relatively recent. Also from textbooks and other related book sources. Conference proceedings are another important source of information for researchers. Reports from government agencies, corporations, commissions are also reliable sources of information for researchers. Also theses and dissertations can rely upon as informative sources.

## Plagiarism in literature review

Plagiarism is the act of copying directly or reshuffling an idea or fact available in literature without acknowledging or crediting the original writer through citation, quotation, or referencing. In other words, when a researcher puts down someone else's expression or thought as though it were his own. A more specific explanation were put forward by Jill & Fiona in this way: "*Plagiarism of words happens when you copy another author exactly without putting the words in italics or quotation marks. Even if you provide reference information you still need to put the text in quotation marks or italics. Where you make quotations you must give the page number.*" This is an unethical act that denotes a grave offence in the academic community. In extreme cases, it is regarded is a sack-able offence, depending on the laws guiding the institution. Here are some ways to avoid plagiarism.

1. First and foremost, try to avoid the temptation of being careless and forgetful of the sources of the research materials. Put

differently, ensure you carefully identify and keep the research materials used in your work.
2. Acknowledge any paraphrased idea or exact word for word of the original writers, through citation and referencing.
3. Put the original writer's exact expression in italics or quotation marks.
4. Plagiarism software should be used to check the work of the researcher to know whether he meets the required plagiarism minimum.

## References

Skolimowski, H. (1967) : "Knowledge and man." The Journal of New paradigm Research. Volume 6. Issue 1, pp 1.

Hart, C. (1998). *Doing a Literature Review.* London: Sage Publications

Hart, C. (2001). *Doing a Literature Review.* London: SAGE: 31

Jankowitz, A. D. (1995). Business research projects. London: Chapman Hill. In Saunders M., Lewis P., & Thornhill A. pp. 128-9

USC Libraries. (n.d.) Organizing Your Social Sciences Research Paper. Retrieved from http://libguides.usc.edu/writringguide/literaturereview.

University of Kent UELT, Student Learning Advisory Service. www.kent.ac.uk/learning

University of the Fraser Valley, counseling department. Student services. www.ufv.ca/studentservices.

Jesson, J., and Lacey, F. (2006). "Pharmacy Education." 6(2): 139 - 148

Skills for Learning (2018) *Guide to report writing* [online] Wolverhampton: University of Wolverhampton [Access date] Available from <http://www.wlv.ac.uk/skills>.

Emerald Group Publishing (n.d.) How to Write a Literature Review. Retrived from http://www.emeraldgrouppublishing.com/authors/guides/write/literature.htm.

Ramdhan, A., Ramdhani, M. A., and Abdusy Syakur Amin, A. S. (2014). "Writing a literature review research paper: A step-by-step approach." International Journal of Basic and Applied Science, Vol. 03, No. 01, July 2014, pp. 47-56

# CHAPTER FIVE

# METHODS OF DATA COLLECTION IN SOCIAL AND LEGAL RESEARCH

**Clement Odiri Obagbinoko**

## Introduction

This chapter explains the various techniques and methods that researchers deploy to generate data in social and legal research. Also the chapter discusses the intricacies of data gathering, the effects of ecological and other extraneous factors on the process of data collection, and the effects of human and material variables on the choice of the technique of data gathering in social and legal research.

Generally speaking, every researcher requires data which are regarded as the raw materials for research. The word data is the plural form of *datum* which in everyday manner of speaking refers to information, facts in a form that can be stored and retrieved for subsequent or future use (Biereenu-Nnabugwu, 2006). While Anikpo in Biereenu-Nnabugwu (2006) equates data with information, Okeke in Biereenu-Nnabugwu (2006) sees data as quantitative information that is utilized to test hypotheses. However, Okeke's attempt in trying to tie data strictly to quantitative information underscores the inadequacy of his definition. Thus, in a more embracing definition, Onu in Biereenu-Nnabugwu (2006) points out that "data is quantitative and qualitative information obtained from varying sources for the purpose of analysis and generalization." Murgan (2015) refers to data as the information, facts, observation, measurements or materials that are collected by a researcher for the purpose of generating results for his research.

In the *Reference Model for an Open Archival Information System (OAIS)*, data is defined as "a reinterpretable representation of information in a formalized manner suitable for communication, interpretation, or processing. Examples of data include a sequence of bits, a table of numbers, the characters on a page, the recording of sounds made by a person speaking, or a moon rock specimen." (What is data, n.d.). also, research data has been defined "as recorded factual material commonly retained by and accepted in the scientific community as necessary to validate research findings; although the majority of such data is created in digital format, all research data is included irrespective of the format in which it is created." (What is research data, 2019). Thus, some essential elements of data can be identified as follows:

- Data is an assembled and ordered system of facts
- Data can be gathered qualitatively and quantitatively from various sources
- The purpose of gathering research data is to conduct or carry out analysis
- Data expectedly result in generalization if properly analysed.

From the foregoing, it can be inferred that research data, unlike other types of information, is collected, observed, or created, for purposes of analysis to produce original research results.

However, attempts have been made by some scholars to define data by taking a look at what data is NOT. This they did by looking at the following:

- preliminary analyses
- drafts of scientific papers
- plans for future research
- peer reviews, or communications with colleagues
- physical objects (e.g., laboratory samples)
- trade secrets
- commercial information
- materials necessary to be held confidential by a researcher until they are published, or similar information which is protected under law (What is data, n.d.).

It is interesting to note that there appears to be an appreciable level of consensus on the definition of data. However, research data vary according to discipline and according to the research funder. Therefore, the method of data collection is largely determined by the type of data to be generated. We shall briefly discuss the major types of data below.

## Types of Data

Generally speaking, data are organised into two broad categories: qualitative and quantitative. However, our discussion here will also be extended to primary and secondary data.

**Qualitative Data:** Qualitative data are mostly non-numerical and are usually descriptive or nominal in nature. This means the data collected are in the form of words and sentences. Often (not always), such data captures feelings, emotions, or subjective perceptions of something. Essentially, qualitative data refers to attributes that cannot be measured numerically. Therefore, when people or things are sorted in groups with each possessing some attributes that cannot be measured numerically, such data collection process gives rise to qualitative data. For example, when a population or sample is classified on the basis of gender into male or female; on the basis of marital status into married or single; or on the basis of occupation, political leanings or religion, qualitative classification of data becomes the inevitable outcome (Biereenu-Nnabugwu, 2006; Kabir, 2016).

Qualitative data represent certain characteristics or attributes to the extent that they depict descriptions that may be observed but cannot be computed or calculated. For example, data on attributes such as *intelligence, honesty, wisdom, cleanliness, and creativity* collected using the students of your class as sample would be classified as qualitative. They are more exploratory than conclusive in nature (Statistics data, (n.d.).

**Quantitative Data:** Quantitative classification of data is hinged on the belief that it is possible to isolate and to test the empirical aspect of our beliefs about politics without necessarily going into the value-laden question of whether the empirical propositions are true or false. Thus, when items vary to the extent that they can be measured or counted, they are referred to quantitative data (Biereenu-Nnabugwu, 2006) Quantitative data is numerical in nature and can be mathematically computed. Quantitative data measure uses different scales, which can be classified as nominal scale, ordinal scale, interval scale and ratio scale. Often (not always), such data includes measurements of something. Examples of quantitative data are Age, Height, Income, Examination scores, Number of children etc (Kabir, 2016). Quantitative data can be measured and not simply observed. They can be numerically represented and calculations can be performed on them. For example, data on the number of students playing different sports from your class gives an estimate of how many of the total students play which sport. This information is numerical and can be classified as quantitative (Statistics data, (n.d.).

The major difference between quantitative data and qualitative data is that while the former is variables-oriented the latter is attributes-oriented. Variables lend themselves to mathematical treatment while attributes do not. To do a credible and quantitative inclined research, hypotheses are stated in quantifiable terms. For example, the statement *Nigeria has more soldiers than Cameroon* will certainly be more amenable to empirical or quantitative test than say *Nigeria is more powerful than Cameroon* (Biereenu-Nnabugwu, 2006).

**Primary Data**: These are data that are *collected for the first time* by an investigator for a specific purpose. Primary data are 'pure' in the sense that no statistical operations have been performed on them and they are original. An example of primary data is census figure (Statistics data, n.d.). Primary data have also been described as data that have been collected from first-hand-experience. Primary data are considered not to have been published yet and are therefore more reliable, authentic and objective. Primary data has not been changed or altered by human beings; therefore its validity is greater than secondary data. In statistical surveys, it is necessary to get information from primary sources and work on primary data. For example, the statistical records of female population in a country cannot be based on newspaper, magazine and other printed sources (Kabir, 2016).

**Secondary Data**: These are data that are *sourced from someplace* that has originally collected it. This means that this kind of data have already been collected by some researchers or investigators in the past and is available either in published or unpublished form. This information is impure as statistical operations may have been performed on them already. An example is information available on government official records, website or in other repositories, books, journals, etc. (Statistics data, (n.d.). In other words, data collected from a source that has already been published in any form is called as secondary data (Kabir, 2016).

## Methods of Data Collection in Social Science

What is data collection and what does method of data collection mean? Murgan (2015) defines data collection as the process of collecting and measuring information on variables of interest in an established systematic manner that enables one to answer stated research question, test hypothesis and evaluate outcome, while the methods of data gathering are the techniques, instruments and approaches that are used for data collection by a researcher. However, the method of data gathering in the social and behavioural science depends on the type of data that a researcher actually requires; whether it is primary data or secondary data. In primary data collection, you collect the data yourself using qualitative and quantitative methods. The key point here is that the data you collect is unique to you and your research and, until you publish, no one else has access to it. There are numerous methods of collecting primary data in social science research; however, for the purpose of this work we shall restrict our discussion to four major methods of data collection. They are:

- Observation
- Survey
- Content Analysis
- Focus Group Discussion (FGD)

These methods will now be discussed one after the other.

## Observation

According to Ojo (1997), observation is a routine of our daily life, but observation of everyday life is haphazard hence the emphasis on scientific observation which is mainly defined by its systematic procedures. Observation technique is commonly used in studies relating to behavioural science. Under this method, observation becomes a scientific tool and the method of data collection for researchers when it serves a formulated research purpose and is systematically planned and subjected to checks and control (Methods of data collection-primary and secondary data, n.d.).

It is interesting to note that much of social science research is rooted in observation and to every investigator observations at first hand are the most satisfactory. Observation as a data collection process entails sight and visual engagement of the researcher. The researcher selects and subjects the phenomenon or activity he wishes to investigate to visual observation and systematically records relevant information or evidence obtained during the observational process. Quite often, information obtained from observation may include those derived from human senses such as hearing, touch or smell. Visual information are however the most commonly applied by data from observational method in social science research (Ojo, 1997)

Observation as a method of data collection is classified into two types:- the first category relates to the extent of structure of the environment in which the observation is being conducted. The research environment may be either natural setting or artificial setting i.e. experimental setting. The second classification of the observational method relates to the degree of structure imposed on the observational environment by the researcher. The distinction here is on whether the observation is either structured of unstructured. The observational technique could be conducted either in form of participant observation or non-participant observation. Participant observation relates to observational research procedures in which the researcher may himself participate actively in the group activity or situation being studied. The participant technique entails a high degree of personal contact of the researcher with the observed and maximizes the opportunity where the observer shares the experiences of the observed. Under the non-participant observer category, the investigator may remain purely as an observer without participating directly in the situation under investigation (Ojo, 1997)

## Survey

The survey method could serve as a useful alternative for the observational method of data gathering. For example, where a phenomenon is not accessible for direct observation, researchers find it necessary to resort to other data generating techniques like the survey method. The main rational for the use of survey method in social science research as a against observational method has been well summarized by G. W Allport as follows: “if we want to know how people feel, what they experience and what they remember, what their emotions and their motives are like, and the reason for acting as they do – why not ask them?" (Ojo, 1997).

In a survey research method of data collection, questions are addressed to a representative (or sample) of population relevant to a research problem or question. The persons to whom questions are addressed in a survey are called respondents. Surveys are generally conducted on the basis of samples as it is practically impossible to obtain the responses of everyone in the population (Ojo, 1997).

Survey method consists of two main data collection instruments. They are Questionnaire and Interview. Although some authors prefer to treat the questionnaire and interview separately as methods of data collection, they are in fact categories of data collection instruments under the survey method. When the instrument is administered directly to the respondent to be filled by him or herself without the assistance of an interviewer, the instrument is called a questionnaire. On the other hand, when the data collection instrument is not given directly to the respondent but filled in by an interviewer who reads the questions to the respondent, it is called an interview schedule.

## Questionnaire

Kabir, (2016) refers to questionnaire as a research instrument consisting of a series of questions and other prompts for the purpose of gathering information from respondents. Although they are often designed for statistical analysis of the responses, this is not always the case. The questionnaire was invented by Sir Francis Galton (1822 - 1911). The unique feature of a questionnaire is that the questions are uniform and typed. Usually, a questionnaire consists of a number of questions that the respondent has to answer in a set format. In a questionnaire, distinction is made between open-ended and closed-ended questions. An open-ended allows the respondent the freedom to choose his/her responses. In other words, the question requires the respondent to formulate his/her own answer. For example, a researcher may ask: **why do you think Western Democracies are critical of Military regimes in Africa?** Then a space is provided for the respondent to answer the question. Whereas in closed-ended question, the respondent is required to select his/her answers from a list provided by the researcher. Example of close-ended question is: **Female students are more diligent: Agree [ ] Agree strongly [ ] Disagree [ ] Disagree strongly [ ] Neutral [ ]**. The response options for a closed-ended question should be exhaustive and mutually exclusive. The questions are designed so that they address specific aspects of the research questions, hypotheses and some other relevant part. The foregoing agrees with Biereenu-Nnabugwu's categorization of questionnaire into three types which are *Structured questionnaire, Unstructured questionnaire and Pictorial questionnaire* (Kabir, 2016; Osemwota, 1996; Biereenu-Nnabugwu, 2006).

The structured questionnaire is the pre-coded type of questionnaire in which respondents respond to questions by restricting themselves to options listed by the researcher. Structured questionnaire include the *dichotomous* questions which contains two-option check mark responses from which a respondent makes a choice. Good examples are questions on gender, marital status, viz

What is your gender (sex)? Male [ ] Female [ ]

Marital status: Married [ ] single [ ]

The *Trichotomous* questions provide a list of three suggested responses. Example is

Which faith do you profess?

Christianity [ ]

Islam [ ]

Others [ ]

The Multi-choice questions provide many choices from which the respondent can choose. E.g.

What is your marital status? Single [ ] Married [ ] Divorced [ ] Widowed [ ] Separated [ ] (Biereenu-Nnabugwu, 2006).

Unstructured questionnaire consist essentially of open-ended questions in which response is unstructured. Under the unstructured questionnaire, respondents are free to respond in the way and manner they like. Example of unstructured questionnaire is:

Where do you reside? ________________________________ or

What is your occupation? ________________________________

The questions above allow the respondents the freedom and latitude to respond the way they like.

Pictorial questionnaire are presented in pictorial format to the effect that respondents are expected to make their choices guided by photographs, drawings or symbols. Example:

Which of the following political party did you vote for during the 2015 general elections?

------------------------ **All Progressive Party**

------------------------ **People's Democratic Party**

------------------------ **Action Alliance**

**Bierrenu-Nnabugwu (2006)**

Questionnaires have advantages over some other types of surveys in that they are cheap, do not require as much effort from the questioner as in verbal or telephone surveys, and often have standardized answers that make it simple to compile data. Other advantages of the questionnaire instrument include the following:

1. Less skill is required – the administration of questionnaire does not require special skill.
2. Saves time and effort compared with the face-to-face interview process.
3. Wide coverage – so many people and wide area can be reached through the questionnaire method.
4. Guarantees greater anonymity – unlike interviews which identifies the respondents physically, the questionnaire does not require the physical presence of the respondents. This also means that respondents are likely to respond to questions without due influence.
5. Easy to format – information gathered from questionnaire is often easy to format in a standardizes manner.
6. Information gathered from questionnaire can easily be quantified and analysed.

## Disadvantages of questionnaire

1. Phenomenologists believe that quantitative research is simply an artificial creation by the researcher, as it is asking only a limited amount of information without explanation.
2. Collusion by respondents – questionnaire method of data gathering is susceptible to inaccuracy arising from collusion by respondents.
3. Amenable to misinterpretation – on account of a variety of reasons, gathering research data through the use of questionnaire method is often susceptible to misinterpretation. Inspite of the effort by the researcher to ensure that the questions unambiguous, the questions may still not be clear to the respondents and indeed may be misinterpreted by the respondents.
4. There is no way to tell how truthful a respondent is being.
5. There is no way of telling how much thought a respondent has put in.
6. The respondent may be forgetful or not thinking within the full context of the situation.
7. People may read differently into each question and therefore reply based on their own interpretation of the question - i.e. what is 'good' to someone may be 'poor' to someone else, therefore there is a level of subjectivity that is not acknowledged.

Questionnaires are not among the most prominent methods in qualitative research, because they commonly require subjects to respond to a stimulus, and thus they are not acting naturally (Kabir, 2016; Biereenu-Nnabugwu, 2006).

## Interview

Although, both the interview and questionnaire instruments are considered to be effective methods in obtaining information about personal perceptions, beliefs, feelings, motivations, anticipations or future plans as well as past behaviour, the interview instrument is believed to be more effective as it ensures that questions are well communicated and better understood while the responses are properly recorded (Kabir, 2016). The interview method of data collection is a face-to-face, verbal and non-verbal communication between the investigator and his or her sample/population. Interview instrument provides an on the spot opportunity for the researcher (interviewer) to administer on, elicit and obtain information from the respondent (interviewee). This method is unlike the questionnaire which though administered by the researcher, but recorded by the respondent himself. Interview instrument enables an interviewer have deeper knowledge about issues of concern through verbal and non-verbal interface with the interviewee (Biereenu-Nnabugwu, 2006).

Biereenu-Nnabugwu (2006) identifies four types of interview. They are:

*Single or individual interview* – this refers to the type of interview directed at one person or individual. In other words, only one person is interviewed.

*Group interview* – this entails bringing together of appropriate persons with varied view points, common or divergent backgrounds to tackle the same problem at a time. This type of interview is likely to produce a more balanced and useful information although considered more costly compared with the single interview.

*Structured interview* – also known as formal interview, structured interview are interviews which the structures of the questions are substantially standardized and formalized. The questions are structured in such a way that uniform set of questions are being asked. Structured interview is largely quantitative in nature and its analysis is more straight forward.

*Unstructured interview* – as the name implies, this type of interview is essentially informal and the interviewer is at liberty to vary or adjust the questions. Unstructured interview often makes use of open-ended questions such that the interviewer is free to determine the questions to ask. It also encourages free expression particularly for the interviewee.

Kabir (2016) and Biereenu-Nnabugwu (2006) explain other advantages of the interview instrument are as follows:

1. It does not require specific level of education for a respondent to participate. Thus information can be gathered from a large number of people including literates and illiterates.

2. Interviews can be done informally, and 'on the fly' and, therefore, do not require scheduling time with respondents. In fact, respondents may just see this as 'conversation'
3. Informal interviewing can be helpful in building rapport with respondents and in gaining their trust as well as their understanding of a topic, situation, setting, etc.
4. Informal interviews, like unstructured interviews, are an essential part of gaining an understanding of a setting and its members' ways of seeing. It can provide the foundation for developing and conducting more structured interviews.
5. Interviews are a far more personal form of research than questionnaires.
6. Unlike with mail surveys, the interviewer has the opportunity to probe or ask follow up questions.

### Disadvantages of interview

1. The use of the interview instrument to gather data can be expensive because the tendency is for the researcher to reach every respondent personally.
2. It is time consuming and energy sapping. A lot of time is usually spent in trying to make contact with prospective respondents and arrange for an interview session.
3. Planning and executing interviews requires specific skills. It is not an all-comers affair. If the skill is lacking, the rate of collection and quality of data collected will be adversely affected.
4. The attitude and mood of both the interviewer and interviewee can have adverse effect the interview process.
5. Respondents in an interview process may due to circumstances known to him give false information. Similarly, due to time factor or due to the fact that his confidentiality is threatened, respondents may give inaccurate information or information that is at variance with their opinion.

## Content Analysis

There is a raging controversy particularly among undergraduate and post graduate researchers regarding the status of content analysis whether as a data collection instrument or a data analysis instrument. However, there is a preponderance of opinion that content analysis serves both as a data collection instrument as well as an instrument of data analysis. White (1983) further clarifies that content analysis enables a political inquirer "to scrutinize the content of a document in order to understand its underlying structures, ideas and concepts and to qualify the message it relates." Thus, according to Kripendoff (1980) content analysis can be referred to as "the systematic reading of a body of texts, images, and symbolic matter, not necessarily from an author's or user's perspective." Content analysis is distinguished from other kinds of social science research in that it does not require the collection of data from people. Like documentary research, content analysis is the study of recorded information or information which has been recorded in texts, media or physical items.

Content analysis is essentially a factor or an extension of documentary and observation instruments of data generation. It focuses at the thorough examination of documents in order to generate information for inference based on the canons of scientific research. In other words, researchers who are interested in a more scientifically rigorous and quantitative analysis of documents generally adopt the content analysis approach. Basically, the content analysis method of data generation takes a verbal, qualitative document and transforms it into quantitative data. This is to the extent that the results derived from content analysis can be presented in percentages, graphs and in tabular format (Osemwota, 1996; Biereenu-Nnabugwu, 2006).

The content that is analysed can be in any form to begin with, but is often converted into written words before it is analysed. The original source can be printed publications, broadcast programs, other recordings, the internet, or live situations. All this content is something that people have created. You cannot do content analysis of (say) the weather - but if somebody writes a report predicting the weather, you can do a content analysis of that (Know your audience: Content analysis, n.d.)

Osemwota (1997) emphasizes that content analysis is a structured – document – analysis technique in which the researcher first constructs a set of manually exclusive and exhaustive categories that can be used to analyze documents and then records the frequency with which each of these categories is observed in the document studied. For example, a researcher may be interested in doing a study on whether or not the *Punch* newspaper was anti the People's Democratic Party (PDP) for the period the party was in power at the centre. The starting point may be to collate all the *Punch* newspapers published between 1999 and 2015 when the PDP was in power. This may serve as the sample of study for the researcher. Based on this sample, the researcher may proceed to study all the editorials /opinion pages of the sample with the intention to score them with regard to whether they were anti or pro the PDP. The researcher can then present his data in tables or in a quantitative format for analysis.

## Focus Group Discussion

Focus group discussion (FGD) is frequently used as a qualitative approach to gain an in-depth understanding of social issues. The method aims to obtain data from a purposely selected group of individuals rather than from a statistically representative sample of a broader population. Even though the application of this method in conservation research has been extensive, there are no critical assessments of the application of the technique. In addition, there are no readily available guidelines for conservation researchers (Nyumba, Wilson, Derrick & Mukherjee, 2018).

A focus group discussion is thus an in-depth field method that brings together a small homogeneous group (usually six to twelve persons) to discuss topics on a study agenda. Usually, the purpose of the FGD is to use the social dynamics of the group, with the help of a moderator/facilitator, to stimulate participants to reveal underlying opinions, attitudes, and reasons for their behavior. It is believed that a well facilitated group can be helpful in finding out the 'how' and 'why' of human behavior. Focus group discussions are a data collection method where data is collected through a semi-structured group interview process. Focus groups are generally used to collect data on a specific topic. Focus group methods emerged in the 1940s with the work of Merton and Fiske who used focus groups to conduct consumer satisfaction. The discussion is conducted in a relaxed atmosphere to enable participants express themselves without any personal inhibitions. Participants usually share a common characteristic such as age, sex, or socio-economic status that defines them as a member of a target subgroup. This encourages a group to speak more freely about the subject without fear of being judged by others thought to be superior. The discussion is led by a trained moderator/facilitator (preferably experienced), assisted by an observer who takes notes and arranges any tape recording (Kabir, 2018).

The popularity of the FGD method of data collection is closely linked to the rise of participatory research, especially the "active experimentation with focus groups" in the academic social sciences during the 1980s. The technique emerged as a qualitative data collection approach and a bridging strategy for scientific research and local knowledge. Focus group discussion is perceived to be a "cost-effective" and "promising alternative" in participatory research offering a platform for differing paradigms or worldviews. However, the popularity of FGD and its application has grown across a wide range of disciplines including education, communication and media studies, sociology, feminist research, health research and marketing research (Nyumba et al, 2018).

Focus group discussion is sometimes seen as synonymous with interviews, especially the semi-structured "one-to-one" and "group interviews" However, existing evidence on the role of the researcher and the relationship with the participants points to a fundamental difference between the two techniques. Interviews involve a one-to-one, qualitative and in-depth discussion where the researcher adopts the role of an "investigator." This implies the researcher asks questions, controls the dynamics of the discussion, or engages in dialogue with a specific individual at a time. In contrast, in a focus group discussion, researchers adopt the role of a "facilitator" or a "moderator." In this setting, the researcher facilitates or moderates a group discussion between participants and not between the researcher and the participants. Unlike interviews, the researcher thereby takes a peripheral, rather than a centre-stage role in a focus group discussion (Nyumba et al, 2018).

## Types of Focus Group Discussion

Nyumba et al, (2018) outline the various types of focus group discussion as follows:

1. *Single focus group* - The key feature of a single focus group is the interactive discussion of a topic by a collection of all participants and a team of facilitators as one group in one place. This is the most common and classical type of focus group

discussion. This type has been widely used by both researchers and practitioners across different disciplines

2. *Two-way focus group* - This format involves using two groups where one group actively discusses a topic, whereas the other observes the first group. Usually, this type of focus group is conducted behind a one-way glass. The observing group and the moderator can observe and note the interactions and discussion of the first group without being seen. Hearing what the other group thinks (or by observing their interactions) often leads the second group to different conclusions than those it may have reached otherwise.
3. *Dual moderator focus group* – This involves two moderators working together, each performing a different role within the same focus group. The division of roles ensures a smooth progression of the session and ensures that all topics are covered.
4. *Dueling moderator focus group* - This involves two moderators who purposefully take opposing sides on an issue or topic under investigation. Proponents believe that the introduction of contrary views to the discussion by the moderators is critical to achieving more in-depth disclosure of data and information.
5. *Respondent moderator focus group* - In this type of focus group discussion, researchers recruit some of the participants to take up a temporary role of moderators. Having one of the participants lead the discussion is thought to impact on the dynamics of the group by influencing participants' answers, thereby increasing the chances of varied and more honest responses.

The Focus Group Discussion instrument is a systematic method of data gathering and there are stipulated guidelines for conducting FGD in social research. Kabir (2016) provides the following guidelines for conducting FGD.

1. **Selection of topic:** It is appropriate to define and clarify the concepts to be discussed. The basic idea is to lay out a set of issues for the group to discuss. It is important to bear in mind that the moderator will mostly be improvising comments and questions within the framework set by the guidelines. By keeping the questions open-ended, the moderator can stimulates

useful trains of thought in the participants that were not anticipated.

2. **Selecting the study participants:** Given a clear idea of the issues to be discussed, the next critical step in designing a focus group study is to decide on the characteristics of the individuals who are to be targeted for sessions. It is often important to ensure that the groups all share some common characteristics in relation to the issue under investigation. If you need to obtain information on a topic from several different categories of informants who are likely to discuss the issue from different perspectives, you should organize a focus group for each major category. For example a group for men and a group for women, or a group for older women and group for younger women. The selection of the participants can be on the basis of purposive or convenience sampling. The participants should receive the invitations at least one or two days before the exercise. The invitations should explain the general purpose of the FGD.
3. **Physical arrangements:** Communication and interaction during the FGD should be encouraged in every way possible. Arrange the chairs in a circle. Make sure the area will be quite, adequately lighted, etc., and that there will be no disturbances. The FGD preferably should take place in a neutral setting that would encourage participants to freely express their views. A health center, for example, is not a good place to discuss traditional medical beliefs or preferences for other types of treatment. Neutral setting could also be from the perspective of a place where the participants feel comfortable to come over and above their party factions.

It should be noted that the role of the researcher/facilitator is very critical to the focus group discussion method and the success of a well conducted focus group discussion exercise largely depends on the skill and training of the group facilitator and team members. Also, it is believed that the rate of unbiased data collection is a function of skillful facilitation.

One of the benefits of focus group discussion is that it is a flexible technique of data collection and it is adaptable at any stage of the research. Compared to more conventional techniques such as individual interviews and surveys, focus group discussion offers an opportunity to explore issues that are not well understood. According to Nyumba et al. (2018) focus group discussion, as a qualitative research method, is comparatively easier to conduct since all the target participants and the researcher are readily available in one location at the same time. Geographic proximity is an important consideration for researchers with resources constraints in developing nations.

However, some of the shortcomings of the FGD are: focus group participants are sometimes reluctant to deal with sensitive topics in a discussion setting compared with an individual interview or a survey; the number of participants to be invited to a focus group discussion interview is hardly determined. This uncertainty is due to the lack of guarantee that all those recruited will attend the discussion. Although it is generally accepted that between six and eight participants are sufficient, some studies have reported as few as four and as many as fifteen participants (Nyumba et al, 2018).

## Method of Data Collection in Legal Research

The method of data gathering in legal research is determined by the research method chosen by the researcher. However, legal research process is performed between two common methods i.e., doctrinal and empirical methods. Thus, the method of data gathering in legal research depends on whether the research is doctrinal or empirical in nature. According to Kharel (2018), doctrinal legal research comprises in-depth analysis of the legal doctrine with its development process and legal reasoning whereas non-doctrinal or empirical research seeks various social facts, relationship of law with those facts, impact of law on society and such. Given that it has gained wider acceptance from all quarters of legal professionals, namely the lawyers, the judges, legal scholars and jurists, doctrinal legal research has remained a prominent research method in law.

At this juncture, it should be noted that the empirical legal method of data collection is virtually the same with the major types of data collection in social science research which have been discussed above. They include the observation and the survey types. Therefore, it will be meaningless and amounts to superfluous discussing them here again. Our main focus here will be on the doctrinal legal research and an attempt on one empirical legal research - the case study research methods of data gathering.

## Data Collection in Doctrinal Research

The concept of doctrinal research is derived from the word 'Doctrine' which means "a principle, especially a legal principle that is widely adhered to." Terry Hutchinson and Nigel Duncan in Kharel (2018) define, the word 'doctrine' as "a word derived from the Latin *doctrina* which means to instruct, a lesson, a precept." They explain that doctrine includes legal concepts and principles of all types – cases, statutes, rules. Doctrine is "a synthesis of rules, principles, norms, interpretive guidelines and values. It explains, makes coherent or justifies a segment of the law as part of a larger system of law. Doctrines can be abstract, binding or non-binding." Based on the observation of these two definitions, we come to know that legal doctrine consists of body of rules associated with legal concept or principle that could have long history of development. Hence, doctrinal legal research is all about thorough enquiry in legal concepts, values, principles and existing legal texts such as statutes, case laws etc (Kharel, 2018).

Vibhute and Aynalem (2009) define doctrinal legal research as research into legal doctrines through analysis of statutory provisions and cases by the application of power of reasoning. Thus it gives emphasis on analysis of legal rules, principles or doctrines. The authors duo compare and contrast doctrinal legal research with non-doctrinal one as follows, "doctrinal legal research endeavours to develop theories, and non-doctrinal legal research endeavours to see as to whether the theories, the doctrines, that we have assumed are appropriate to apply in society at a given time, are still valid and relevant." Doctrinal legal research is, therefore, 'research *in* law' while non-doctrinal legal research is 'research *about* law.' Doctrinal or library-based research is the most common methodology employed by those undertaking research in law. Doctrinal research asks, what is the law in a particular case? It is concerned with the analysis of the legal doctrine and how it was developed and applied (Ali, Yusoff & Ayub, 2017).

Doctrinal legal research is distinguished from other non-doctrinal legal researches on the basis of data employed during the study. Doctrinal research is always based on secondary data that come from authorities. Though data can be retrieved from both primary and secondary authorities, doctrinal research never deals with the primary data of social facts collected first-hand from surveys, field study or any other empirical means. Doctrinal researcher analyses available secondary data from authoritative sources which have already been collected and processed by other else than the researcher. In doctrinal research, usually researcher analyses secondary available data, which come from statutes, laws, judicial decisions and other legal texts, to verify the legal proposition and reach to a conclusion. Doctrinal legal research gets its data basically from authoritative sources, either from law itself or legal texts having some sense of sovereign or authority in it. Most of the legal scholars consequently prefer doctrinal research due to its hassle free nature – not required to wander various places to gather first-hand information from field studies (Kharel, 2018).

Much of the traditional approach for legal research revolves round the doctrinal method; even today doctrinal method is first choice of the researchers in law schools. The domain of doctrinal research mostly makes use of the following techniques of data collection:

*Library Research* - Legal theories, principles and position of law may be easily referred by sitting in the library. Contents of the documents are self sufficient to be shown as good evidence of what law is on any issue of law and society, explanations, and object of law can be referred by bare reading of texts. That is why library research is most convenient way of data collection. Sources of data available within library are - Books, Journals, Reporters, Magazines, News Papers, Juristic work, Reports of (Seminar, conferences, symposiums, legislative, judicial and administrative proceedings), literature containing factual & philosophical information, Articles, Research papers, Thesis and Dissertations, Reports of Commissions, Court judgments and Case commentaries etc. General source materials relating to problem, their background knowledge and knowledge of previous findings in similar cases is easily read in numerable available material in the library. Use of library is a desideratum for law researchers. Researchers who are interested in using library technique firstly, search basic key terms in body of contents, subject index and glossary provided in the text sources. Use of e-library is a modern and advance culture of legal research which is a more efficient way to search on research material by pushing your figures on computer, Laptop and smart phones. Web source and print source are the basics to build up library researches.

*Participation* - Participation technique is another common pattern of data collection in doctrinal as well as in empirical researches. Doctrinal studies can be performed by using either Library, participation or both techniques. The objective of Doctrinal-participative approach is to obtain knowledge by participating in any activity where relevant information may be obtain from verbal statements and presentations made by the persons credible for such information as expert, experienced or authoritative, not from the printing or web materials. It may be obtained by participations in lectures, seminars, conferences, and proceedings of (Academic, Administrative, Judicial and Legislative). Here the objective of participation for doctrinal research is only to receive information given by credible person relevant to study not to observe and analyze the source of information, like observation of source under empirical method. Participation for data collection may be face to face or by modern means of technology i.e., video conferencing, Television, means of mass media and other means of communications (Research methodology methods of data collection, n.d.)

The hallmark of the doctrinal research begins with the developing of a legal proposition by the researcher who then embarks on the analysis of the data from primary and secondary authorities towards testing the proposition. For example, while initiating a doctrinal legal research on the issues of precedents, a legal researcher can construct a proposition that more than two third of the precedents set by the Supreme Court lack convincing legal reasoning behind them. The researcher needs to study bulk of data generated from primary and secondary authorities related to case laws or the contents of the precedents set by Supreme Court within certain timeframe, prior studies on such precedents, related authoritative books and academic writings etc (Kharel, 2018).

The doctrinal legal research method of gathering data is advantageous in several respects. For example, it is often employed in the areas of enriching legal contents, coding and even interpretation of the legal statutes. The doctrinal method is also believed to be highly academic in nature and it is suitable for the purpose of building new principles, adding some new knowledge and providing foundation for study on other various socio-legal issues. Doctrinal legal research boosts confidence of the judges, lawyers and the jurists. A lawyer can do a good legal research in doctrinal approach even during the litigating stage for a particular client (Kharel, 2018).

Although, the doctrinal research method of data gathering has often been referred to as 'armchair' or 'handicapped' type of research, conducting doctrinal research is not such an easy task since it comprises the systematic process of locating and analysing various authoritative legal texts, case laws and similar nature of prior studies as well (Kharel, 2018).

## Empirical (non-doctrinal) Legal Research - The Case Study Method of Data Collection

Apart from the observational and the survey methods, another important method of data collection in legal research is the case study method. The case study research method has been described as a form of qualitative analysis which entails a careful and complete observation of a person, a situation or an institution. It is a method that seeks to organize social data so as to preserve the unitary character of the social object being studied. Also, case study has been defined as a method of exploring and analyzing the life of a social unit, be it a person, a family, an institution, cultural group or even entire community. In other words, a case study research method, tends to investigate one human individual only or only an episode in first life or it might be a Nation or an epoch of history. The case study research method is a synthesis and entails the interpretation of information about a person and his relationship to his environment collected by means of many techniques. (Choudhury, n.d.).

Case study method falls within the social science discipline and as such has scientific underpinnings. The case study examines phenomena in context, where context and findings cannot be separated. In some instances, case study is used to investigate how actors consider, interpret and understand phenomena (e.g., law, procedure, policy) and therefore allows the researcher to study perceptions of processes and how they influence behaviour, for example to understand judges' sentencing choices etc. This may help to understand how laws are understood, and how and why they are applied and/or misapplied, subverted, complied with or rejected. This can flow back into the legal and policy making processes, court procedure, sentencing, punishment, diversion of offenders etc., and may have a high impact as a result (Webley, 2016). As described so far it is a research method that appears to have a lot in common with experiments and tests of statistical significance. But case study method differs markedly from a big data survey or double-blind experiment in that it seeks explicitly a phenomenon in its natural environment and without means to control for variables, including the behaviour of any participants (Webley, 2016).

As a research method, the case study has its advantages and shortcomings of which researchers should be mindful, especially when it is used as an auxiliary method within the framework of empirical legal research. According to Argyrou (2017), the case study research method offers an advantage to the legal researcher in answering questions of 'how' and 'why.' Although these are not legal questions *per se*, they can be complementary to legal questions. In response to these questions, the legal researcher can use a contemporary set of real-life events data (collected through interviews, documents and observations), rather than legal arguments and theoretical constructs, to examine particular topics. The most commonly acknowledged weakness of the case study research method is that it is believed to be vulnerable in terms of rigour and validity when compared with quantitative numeric studies. The case study research is seen to lack the validity of developing a proper sample of cases and providing objectively verified results. In other words, case study research is believed to provide the space for the researcher's bias to infiltrate the selection of cases and the research results (Argyrou, 2017).

The case study research method is perceived to provide a weak basis for generalization. This opinion is hinged on the fact that a case study research carried out on just a single case is inadequate for a generalization and thus provides only a weak basis for generalizations to an entire or larger population. However, it has also been argued that the case study method can provide a strong basis for the 'analytical generalizations' of theories and theoretical propositions particularly in a process of using 'falsification,' 'rival' or 'deviant' cases or 'a case that runs counter to a rule.' Experience has shown (in contrast to other types of research), that case study research requires more time, more commitment and more financial resources (Argyrou, 2017).

## Characteristics of Case Study Method

(1) *The Study of the Whole Unit.* In this study a large variety of units are selected for study and the size of the unit may be quite large to cover an entire community. In a word this method treats an individual, an institution or a group of persons as a whole. This invariably is one of the benefits of case study method of gathering data.

(2) *Intensive Study.* It aims at deep and thorough study of a unit. It deals with every aspect of a unit and studies it intensively (Gosh, n.d.).

According to Gosh (n.d.) two major sources can be applied in the case study method:

(i) Personal Documents - From personal diaries, letters or from autobiographies, the necessary information is collected. The hidden 'secrets of an individual, his way of life, the objects and the mode of life are written in one's personal diary. To this extent, personal documents can be a source of a great deal of information necessary for the study of the problem.

(ii) Life History. In the case study method the life history of a person may be very essential. This can be obtained through interviews with the respondent. In this study the entire life of the respondent is taken into account. The material for the case study can be also gathered from writing materials about the respondent and through interviews. Briefly the entire life cycle of an individual is studied, tested and enquired in this type of case study.

## Limitations of Case Study Method

Like every other data gathering method, the case study method also has its shortcomings. Some of the limitations of the case study method are given below:

1. *False Sense of Confidence.* In case study method a researcher becomes over confident. Since he studies various aspects of the life of an individual he thinks that he knows everything about

that person. But it is seen very often that many other aspects of life were hidden about which the respondent himself was ignorant.

2. *Difficulties in Collection of Historical Data.* Through this method proper data collection is very difficult. This is because generally the respondents do not reveal the actual facts to the researchers.
3. *False Generalization.* Since it is not possible to collect proper data and information through this method the generalizations on this basis become defective and faulty.
4. *Expensive in Nature.* The time and money required for this study are sometimes prohibitive.
5. *Possibility of Error.* There are many chances of making errors in selection of case, observation and so on due to failures of the memory, suppression of unpleasant facts, tendency to exaggerate and the like.
6. *Ad hoc Theorising.* The explanation given through this method is unreliable because the case study method does not give importance to scientific explanation. It emphasises the commonsense explanation. Such explanations are hardly reliable.
7. *Lack of Quantitative Study.* The case study method is qualitative in nature. It deals with only the psychological aspects of a human being. Quantification of the results is not possible in this type of study.
8. *Unorganised and Unsystematic.* The method is unorganised and unsystematic because there is no control on the researcher and on the respondent. Thus verification is not possible. Hence the data collected by this method is often unreliable and the generalization drawn from it is also inaccurate.

## Conclusion

So far, we have been able to explain the meaning of data, the meaning of data gathering and have been able to identify and discuss the various methods of collecting data in the social and legal research. Efforts have been made to identify and discuss the benefits and shortcomings of the various data gathering techniques in the social and legal research. However, it should be noted that data gathering methods in social science research and in legal research are not mutually exclusive. In other words, virtually all the data gathering methods available to researchers in social and behavioural science are also applicable and useful in the legal research. Thus, with regard to methods of data collection, there exists a point of convergence between social and legal research. For example, both the social and legal researchers make use of the observational, survey, interview and case study instruments to generate data.

Taking cognizance of the advantages and limitations of the various data gathering methods discussed above, it is important that adequate care must be taken to ensure that the techniques for data collection are carefully applied and properly managed so as to avoid collation of inaccurate data which may bring about misleading information and poor research result. However, it is recommended that adequate measures be taken to educate researchers (particularly at the undergraduate and postgraduate levels) on the imperatives to distinguish between primary and secondary data and when to apply quantitative and/or qualitative data.

## References

"Statistics data," (n.d.). Retrieved from: https://www.toppr.com/guides/ maths/ statistics/data.

"What is data," (n.d.). University of Minnesota. Retrieved from: https://www.lib.umn.edu/datamanagement

"What is research data" (2019). University of Leicester. Retrieved from: https://www2.le.ac.uk/services/research-data

Ali, S. I.; Yusoff, Z. M. & Ayub, Z. A. (2017). Legal Research of Doctrinal and Non-Doctrinal International *Journal of Trend in Research and Development,* Volume 4(1), ISSN: 2394-9333. Retrieved from: www.ijtrd.com Jan-Feb.

Argyrou, A. (2017). Making the case for case studies in empirical legal research. *Utrecht Law Review*, *Vol. 13, No. 3*, pp. 95-113.

Biereenu-Nnabugwu, M. (2006). Methodology of political inquiry, issues and techniques of research methods in political science. Enugu. Quintagon Publishers.

Choudhury, A. (n.d.). Top 6 Methods of Data Collection – Explained. Retrieved from: http://www.yourarticlelibrary.com

Ghosh, B. N. (n.d) Collection and Analysis of Data. Retrieved from: http://14.139.60.114:8080/jspui/bitstream/123456789/719/35/Collection%20and%20Analysis%20of%20Data.pdf

Kabir, S. M. S. (2016). Methods of data collection. Retrieved from: www.researchgate.net/publication

Kharel, A. (2018) Doctrinal legal research. Available @ http://dx.doi.org /10.2139/ssrn.3130525

Know your audience: Content analysis, (n.d.). Retrieved from: http://www.audiencedialogue.net.

Kripendoff, K. (1980). Content analysis: an introduction to its methodology. Beverly Hills: Sage publications

Methods of data collection - primary and secondary data, (n.d.) Retrieved from: https://bbamantra.com

Murgan, M. G. (2015). A critical analysis of the techniques for data gathering in legal research. *Journal of Social Sciences and Humanities*; Vol. 1, No. 3, 2015, pp. 266-274. Retrieved from: http://www.aiscience.org/journal/jssh

Nyumba, T. O; Wilson, K; Derrick, C. J. & Mukherjee, N. (2018) The use of focus group discussion methodology: Insights from two decades of application in conservation. Retrieved from: https://doi.org/10.1111/2041-210X.12860

Ojo, S. O. J (1997). Sources and techniques of data collection in social science research in V. O. Aghayere and S. O. J. Ojo Ed. Research methods in social science. Benin City. Stirling-Horden Publishers Nig Ltd.

Osemwota, O. (1996). Data collection techniques in Osa Osemwota; M. A. Okhakhu; D. A. Tonwe (Ed) Research and statistical methods. Benin City. UTO Publications

Research methodology: methods of data collection (n.d.). Retrieved from: http://epgp.inflibnet.ac.in.

Vibhute, K. & Aynalem, F. (2009). Legal research methods, *Teaching Material*, Justice and Legal System Research Institute, Ethiopia, 70

Webley, L. (2016). 'Stumbling blocks in empirical legal research: Case study research,' *LaM* October 2016, DOI: 10.5553/REM/.000020

White, L. G. (1990). Political analysis: Technique and practice. California: Brooks/Cole publishing Company

# CHAPTER SIX

# METHODS OF DATA ANALYSIS

**Sylvester Ohiomu**

## Introduction

Data analysis could be defined as a process of cleaning, transforming, and modelling data to reveal the desired information for further usage or business decision-making. The main aim is to extract the needed information from available data and taking vital decision based upon the result obtained. Data analysis is needed to process information, take decision, forecast, grow business and do further analysis.

Data analysis tools make it easier for analysts to process and manipulate data, analyse the relationships and correlations between data sets, and it also helps to ascertain patterns and trends for understanding. Commonly used data analysis tools include: Microsoft Office packages (word, excel, access, power point), SPSS, SQL MATLAB, JAVA, PYTHON, ACL, Microfit, E-views, amongst others

## Types of Data Analysis

Several types of data analysis techniques exist in the learning process based on needs and available technology. In Social Sciences commonly used types of data analysis include: (1) Text Analysis, (2) Statistical Analysis, (3) Diagnostic Analysis, (4) Predictive Analysis and (5) Prescriptive Analysis

### Text Analysis

Text Analysis otherwise called Data Mining, is a method to ascertain a pattern in large data sets using database tools. This method is applied to transform raw data into desired information. Application

Intelligence tools are currently available in the market for analysis to take strategic decisions. Generally, this method offers a technique to extract and scrutinize data and finally interpret the data. It is predominantly used for qualitative data analysis. This recognizes process content and content information in the data mining procedure.

### Statistical Analysis

Statistical Analysis visualises data in an interface driven procedure by using past data in the form of dashboards. Statistical Analysis includes collection, Scrutiny or exploration, interpretation, presentation, and modelling of data. It analyses a set of data or a sample of data. Two categories of Statistical Analysis frequently used in social sciences are descriptive analysis and inferential analysis.

### Descriptive Analysis

Descriptive statistics which deals with methods of organizing, summarizing and presentation of data in a convenient and informative way. Descriptive analysis analyses data or a sample of concise numerical data. It displays mean, median, mode and deviation for continuous data whereas percentage and frequency for definite data.

### Inferential Analysis

Inferential or deductive statistics which deals with methods used to draw conclusion or inferences about the characteristics of populations based on sampled data. Inferential analysis analyses sample from complete data. Using this Analysis, one can draw different conclusions from the same data by selecting diverse samples.

### Diagnostic Analysis

Diagnostic Analysis reveals reason for unique exhibition or trend of data by finding the cause from the insight found in Statistical Analysis. This Analysis is useful to identify behaviour patterns of data. If a new occurrence spurs up in the learning process, Diagnostic Analysis can be used to find similar patterns of that problem which may have chances to use similar prescriptions for the new behaviour.

### Predictive Analysis

Predictive Analysis displays the likely outcome or pattern of occurrence by using previous data. This Analysis makes predictions about future outcomes based on current or past data. Forecasting is just an estimate. Its accuracy is based on how much detailed information you have and how much you dig in it. Similarly, mutations, discovery and new occurrences can affect predictive power of analysis

### Prescriptive Analysis

Prescriptive Analysis pools the comprehension from all previous Analysis to determine which action to take in a current occurrence or decision. Most data-driven researches are applying Prescriptive Analysis because predictive and descriptive Analyses are not enough to improve data performance. Based on current challenges, researchers analyse the data and make decisions for implementation for possible.

### Data Analysis Process

Data Analysis Process is the route or design of gathering information by using proper application or tool which allows you to explore the data and find a pattern in it for meaningful application. Based on the scheme, one can take decisions, or get ultimate conclusions.

Data Analysis consists of the following phases: (1) Data Requirement Gathering, (2) Data Collection, (3) Data Cleaning, (4) Data Analysis, (5) Data Interpretation and (6) Data Visualization

### Data Requirement Gathering

The first thing a researcher considers is the purpose or aim of doing the Analysis before considering which type of data analysis he/she wants to do! In this phase, the researcher decides what to analyse and how to measure it considering the concept under investigation.

### Data Collection

Data is very important in any statistical investigation. After requirement gathering, the researcher should get a clear idea about the content of measurement and the underlining findings. Subsequently, it is time to collect the data based on requirements. After collection, remember that the collected data must be processed or organized for Analysis. As you collected data from various sources, you must have to keep statistics of collection date and source of the data. Various sources of data collection include the following: Primary sources: questionnaire, personal interview, direct interview, registration of events, by telephone amongst others.

Secondary sources: regular records, periodic records and irregular records

Problems of data collection in Nigeria include: secrecy, illiteracy, scanty records, under developed ICT and cumbersome nature of manual data storage

The techniques of collecting primary data known as sampling techniques. These are discussed below.

## Sampling Techniques

Sampling is the process of selecting elements from a given population to make up a sample (a sub-set of a population) for the purpose of research concerning the population.

A population is the totality of the observations with which we are concerned.

In sampling theory only, a part of the population (sample) can provide the necessary information for the researcher to make decisions or inferences, or to test a hypothesis concerning the entire population.

This is done with the risk of errors which can be calculated if the sample is a probability sample.

Two types of sample design include: Probability sample and non-probability sample.

A probability sample is one in which each unit of the population is given some known chance of being selected as part of the sample and hence the error of measurement can be calculated.

The non-probability sample is one in which some units of the population is not given the chance of being selected as part of the sample. In this case, error of measurement cannot be calculated.

There are two basic sampling techniques, methods or designs namely random sampling (Probability sampling) and non-random sampling.

Random sampling is sub-divided into: (a) Simple or unrestricted random sampling, (b) Restricted random sampling classified into: (i) Stratified sampling (ii) Cluster sampling and (iii) Systematic sampling.

Simple or unrestricted random sampling refers to that method of selecting elements from a given population for the purpose of a research, in such a way that every element of the population has equal chance of being selected into the sample. The method is unbiased and not haphazard.

Stratified sampling: In Stratified sampling, preciously heterogeneous population is divided up into homogeneous classes or groups known as strata and then random sampling is applied to each stratum to obtain the needed sample for research.

Stratified sampling is more likely to yield results that are more representative of the population than those of random sampling.

Two types of Stratified sampling include: Proportional and disproportionate.

Proportional Stratified sampling plan is one in which the size of sample drawn from each stratum is proportional to the size of the stratum with respect to the population.

Disproportionate stratified sampling is one in which equal number of elements or samples is drawn from each stratum irrespective of the size of the stratum in the population.

Example: A given population is made up of the police 20%, the Army 50% and the Navy 30%. Determine the number of police, Army and the Navy to be included in a sample of 150 persons (i) if proportional stratified sample is employed (ii) if disproportionate stratified sampling is used.

Solution (i) 3 strata involved and required proportional sample of each stratum are:

| | | |
|---|---|---|
| Stratum 1 (Police) | 150 x 20% = | 30 |
| Stratum 2 (Army) | 150 x 50% = | 75 |
| Stratum 3 (Navy) | 150 x 30% = | 45 |
| Total | | 150 |

(ii) If disproportionate stratified sampling is used then the total sample size should be shared equally between the 3 strata. Thus, each stratum will have 50 persons each.

Cluster Sampling (or Multi-Stage Sampling): The cluster sampling plan involves multiple choice of different samples or the selection of different samples at different stages until a final sample is obtained. Random sampling or any other sampling method may be applied in the selection of the primary, intermediate and final samples. Eg sampling 3600 Nigerian farmers

Systematic (or Quasi-random) Sampling involves the random selection of the very first unit or element of the sample (from among the sampling interval 1 to k) and then the subsequent element are drawn from the population by taking every Kth element (with reference to the first unit) until the entire sample is made up. K is the sampling ratio or sampling interval

$K = N/n$, where $N$ = population size, $n$ = sample size

Non-Random Sampling

Judgement (or Deliberate) Sampling: The Statistician decides which element becomes part of the sample based on what he or she judges to be representative of the population under study.

Quota Sampling: When a population is classified into strata tor the purpose of sampling, the researcher may wish to fix the number of element to be selected from each stratum to make up the sample. The specified number of element to be selected from each stratum are referred to as quotas. The way or manner the quota is filled is at the instance of the researcher's personal judgement. This method of selection is known as quota sampling and it carries high risk of personal prejudice and bias

Convenience (or Chunk) Sampling: In this type of sample design, sample elements are chosen from the population because the elements are readily available or because of the ease or low cost of obtaining the elements.

## Sample Size

Determinants of Sample Size include: The size of the population; The resources available; The nature of the study; The level of accuracy or confidence required

Mathematically, n = {Zδ/d}^2

Where $n$ = sample size, $d$ = difference between sample and population means, $\delta$ = standard deviation of the population to be studied,

Z = confidence level or coefficient determined from the standard normal Table

Example: Given that δ = 200, d = 30, confidence level = 95% Calculate the sample size

Solution: Z = 1.95, Sample size, n = {Zδ/d}^2 = {1.96(200)/30}^2
{13.07}^2 = 170.82

## Data Cleaning

All the data collected may not be 100% useful while some are irrelevant to the aim of Analysis, hence it should be cleaned. The data collected may contain duplicate records, white spaces or errors; hence, the data should be cleaned and error free. This phase must be done properly before Analysis because the expected outcome depends on the extent of data cleaning procedure and its accuracy

## Data Analysis

Once the data is collected, cleaned, and processed, it is ready for Analysis. As the researcher manipulates or analyses the data, the desired information comes up, or the researcher might need to collect more data for further analysis. During this phase, the researcher can use data analysis tools and software which will aid to understand, interpret, and derive conclusions based on the requirements or specifications.

## Data Interpretation

After analysing the data, the researcher needs to interpret the results. The outcome of data analysis can be expressed or communicated either in words or tables or charts. Finally, the researcher can use results of data analysis process to decide on best course of action.

## Data Presentation and Organization

- Forms of presentation of data include the following
- Visual presentation
- Visual Presentation: Examples are (1) tabular presentation with practical demonstration the class (Frequency distribution table)
- (2) Graphical presentation with practical demonstration on graphs (Histogram and frequency polygon)
- (3) Diagrams including bar charts and pie charts

**Multiple Bar Charts**

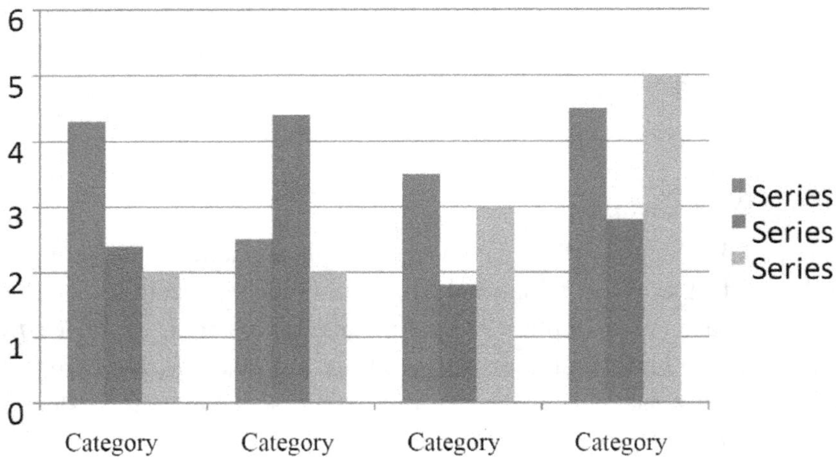


Line Chart

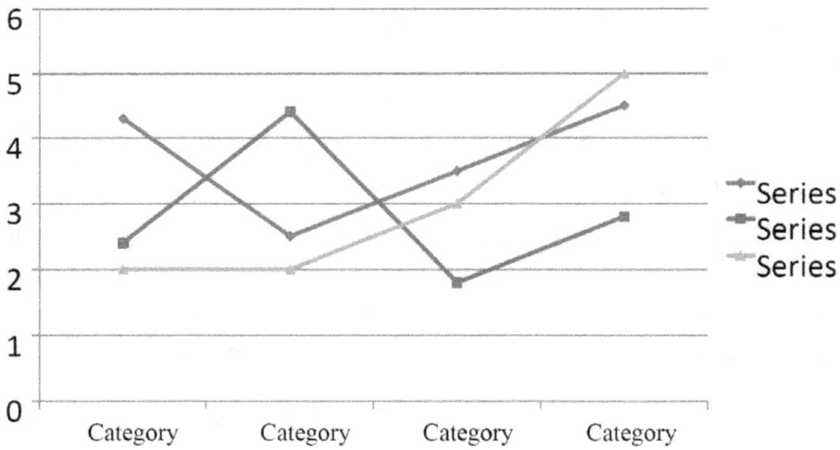

Pie Chart

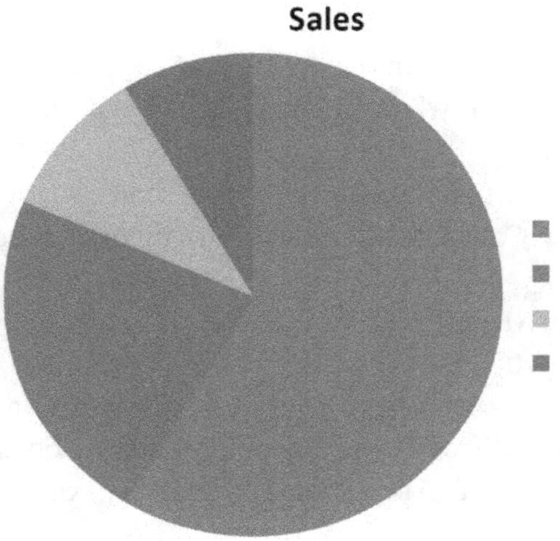


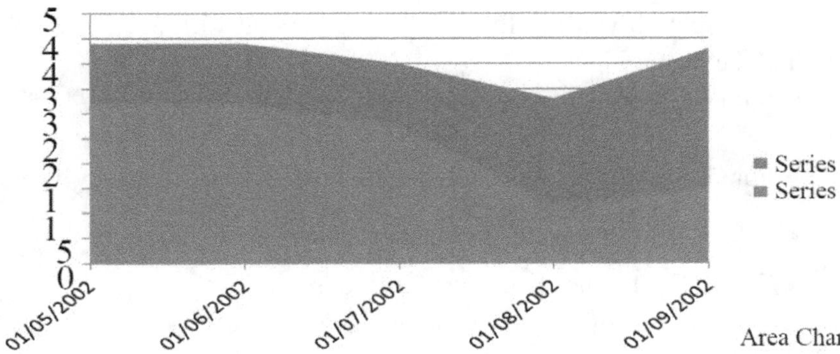


Area Chart

## Data Visualization

Data visualization is very common and useful in daily life application; these visualizations appear in the form of charts and graphs. Interestingly, data can be shown graphically so that it will be easier for the human brain to understand and process it. Data visualization can be used to discover unknown facts and trends. By observing data interactions and comparing datasets, the researcher can find a way to find out meaningful information.

Measure of Central Tendency

Mean

A measure of central tendency is any measure that indicates the centre of distribution which includes the mean, median, mode and Geometric mean.

Mean = "Arithmetic average" of the scores

Example: Calculate the mean of the following scores: 64, 70, 80, 80, 90, 98, 100

Solution: Mean = Sum of values divided by number of scores: 64 + 70 + 80 + 80 + 90 + 98 + 100 = 582 582 ÷ 7 = 83.14

The Mean (Arithmetic Mean) of a finite set of observations is the sum of their values divided by the number of observations

Given a set of observations: x1, x2, …, xn, the mean can be calculated as follows:

$$\ddot{X} = x1 + x2 + \ldots + xn /n = \sum_{i=1}^{n} Xi \, /n$$

Example; Given the following observations 43, 535, 70, 2779, 318. Find the mean

Solution: Mean Ẍ = 43 + 535 + 70 + 2779 + 318 /5 = 3745/5 = 749

For Grouped Data or Calculation of mean from a Frequency Table

$$\ddot{X} = \sum FX / \sum F$$

Where F = frequency or number of observations

Fx = product of frequency and variable

∑F = N = sum of frequencies

Calculation of Mean for Grouped Data is demonstrated in the worked example at the end of this section.

Median

The median is the value of the middle term or value of a series of observation when arrange either in ascending or descending order of magnitude

Take the central number if odd and average of the two central numbers if even observations foe ungrouped data

Median = score in the middle; 50th percentile

Example: Calculate the Median of the following distribution: 64, 70, 80, 80, 90, 98, 100

Solution: if # scores = odd: Find the score in the middle 64, 70, 80, [80], 90, 98, 100

Median = 80

Example: Calculate the Median of the following distribution: 64, 70, 80, 80, 90, 98, 100, 100 Solution: if # scores = even: Average the 2 in the middle 64, 70, 80, [80, 90,] 98, 100, 100

- 80 + 90 = 170 ÷ 2 = 85
- Median = 85

For Grouped data, the Median is given by the formula:

Median = $L + w(n/2 - F_c)/F_e$

Where, L = Lower class boundary of class interval containing the median,

n = total no of observations = $\sum f$

Fc = Cumulative frequency of the class preceding the median class

Fe = Frequency of the class interval containing the median

W = width or size of the median class

Mode

The mode is defined as the observation(s) that occurs with the greatest frequency.

It is possible to have more than one modal value appearing at a time. Thus: One modal value is called Unimodal; Two modal vales = bimodal, Three modal values = trimodal, Four modal values = quadrimodal, Many modal values = multimodal.

- Mode = largest number of scores

Example Calculate the mode of the following distribution: 64, 70, 80, 80, 90, 98, 100

Mode = 80

Example Calculate the mode of the following distribution: 64, 70, 80, 80, 90, 98, 100, 100 Modes = 80, 100. The distribution is bimodal

For Grouped data, the mode is given by the formula:

Mode = L1 + w{(F1 –F0)/[2F1 –F0 –F2]}

Where, L1 = Lower class limit of the modal class

F1 = modal frequency

F0 = Frequency of class immediately preceding the modal class

F2 = Frequency of the class succeeding the modal class

W = Size or width of the modal class

Example: Find the Mean, Median and Mode of the distribution in the table below:

| Class Interval | Frequency |
|---|---|
| 125 -129 | 9 |
| 130 – 134 | 12 |
| 135 – 139 | 21 |
| 140 – 144 | 30 |
| 145 – 149 | 38 |
| 150 – 154 | 20 |
| 155 – 159 | 14 |
| 160 - 164 | 6 |

Solution:

The computed table of distribution is given below:

| Class Interval | Class Mark (X) | Frequency (F) | Cum Freq | FX | |
|---|---|---|---|---|---|
| 125 -129 | 127 | 9 | | 1143 | |
| 130 – 134 | 132 | 12 | 21 | 1584 | |
| 135 – 139 | 137 | 21 | 42 | 2877 | |
| 140 – 144 | 142 | 30 | 72 | 4260 | |
| 145 – 149 | 147 | 38 | 110 | 5586 | Median Class |
| 150 – 154 | 152 | 20 | 130 | 3040 | |
| 155 – 159 | 157 | 14 | 144 | 2198 | |
| 160 - 164 | 162 | 6 | 150 | 972 | |
| | | n = ∑f = 150 | | 21663 | |

Mean = Ẍ = $\sum FX / \sum F$

Where €Fx = product of frequency and variable = 21663

∑F = N = sum of frequencies = 150

- Mean = Ẍ = $\sum FX / \sum F$ =21663/150 = 144.42
- Mean of the distribution is 144.42

Median = L + w(n/2 – $F_c$)/$F_e$

Where, L = Lower class boundary of class interval containing the median = 145

n = total no of observations = ∑f = 150

Fc = Cumulative frequency of the class preceding the median class = 72

Fe = Frequency of the class interval containing the median = 38

W = width or size of the median class = 5

By substitution,

- Median = L + w(n/2 – $F_c$)/$F_e$ = 145 + 5{150/2 – 72}/38
- Median = 145 + 5{75 – 72}38 = 145 + 0.3947 = 145.39
- The Median of the distribution is approximately = 145.39

The mode of the distribution is given by the formula:

Mode = L1 + w{(F1 –F0)/[2F1 –F0 –F2]}

Where, L1 = Lower class limit of the modal class = 145

F1 = modal frequency = 38

F0 = Frequency of class immediately preceding the modal class = 30

F2 = Frequency of the class succeeding the modal class = 20

W = Size or width of the modal class = 5

By substitution into the above formula:

- Mode = L1 + w{(F1 –F0)/[2F1 –F0 –F2]} = 145 + 5{(38 – 30)/(2x38 – 30 – 20)}
- Mode = 145 + 5{8/26} = 145 = 1.538 = 146.54
- The Mode of the distribution is approximately 146.54

Measures of Dispersion (Variation)

The spread of a figure also called the variation tells us how data are dispersed around the mean. There are several measures of dispersion. These include the following:

- Range = Highest observation – lowest observation
- Mean Deviation = average of the deviations of observations from the mean
- Variance = The square of Standard Deviation
- Standard Deviation = σ = Square of Variance
- Coefficient of Variation

Coefficient of Variation

The main items of variation are the mean and standard deviation. It is the relative dispersion and expresses the standard deviation as a percentage of the mean.

Coefficient of variation (CV) = (S.D./Mean) x 100 = ∂/Ẍ x 100%

Coefficient of Mean Deviation = (M.D./Mean) x 100/1

Example: Given the wages of labourers and helpers in a construction firm below: Labourer Ẍ = 2045.50 ∂ = 408.60

Helper Ẍ = 154.25 ∂ = 32.40 Determine the CV and interpret your result

Solution;

V1 = (S.D./Mean) x 100 = ∂/Ẍ x 100 = (408.60/2045.50) x 100 = 19.98%

V2 = (S.D./Mean) x 100 = ∂/Ẍ x 100 = (32.40/154.25) x 100 = 21%

Interpretation: From the result derived above, it is obvious that the wages of labourers are more stable than those of their Helpers since the former has less coefficient of variation (19.98%) than the latter (21.00%)

Econometric Data Analysis Using E-Views

Below is a Summary of Regression Results of Ordinary Least Squares Method from E-views 9 carried out in a lecture with undergraduate students:

Dependent Variable: RGDP
Method: Least Squares
Date: 12/04/19 Time: 11:08
Sample: 1981 2018
Included observations: 38

| Variable | Coefficient | Std. Error | t-Statistic | Prob. |
|---|---|---|---|---|
| C | 1155.139 | 3921.191 | 0.294589 | 0.7701 |
| LINTR | -111.5472 | 218.3065 | -0.510966 | 0.6127 |
| SAVINGS | 0.006945 | 0.000445 | 15.61813 | 0.0000 |
| EXRT | 73.49774 | 22.91133 | 3.207921 | 0.0029 |

| | | | |
|---|---|---|---|
| R-squared | 0.977477 | Mean dependent var | 27569.37 |
| Adjusted R-squared | 0.975490 | S.D. dependent var | 37734.90 |
| F-statistic | 491.8550 | Durbin-Watson stat | 1.544971 |
| Prob(F-statistic) | 0.000000 | | |

**Source: Author's Estimation using E-Views 9**

Analyse the results using econometric data analysis by answering the following questions:

1. Write the final equation from the above results
2. Interpret the significant level of the variables with appropriate consideration to the signs and the overall model
3. How can the Durbin-Watson Statistics be corrected?

Solution:

1. RGDP =1155.139 – 111.5472LINTR+0.006945SAVINGS + 73.49774EXRT
2. The above result implies a positive relationship between RGDP, exchange rate and savings in Nigeria while the lending rate is negatively related to RGDP. Coefficient of Determinant (R2)/Adjusted R2 = 0.977477 and the adjusted R2 = 0.975490. This implies that the mix of regressors; Exchange Rate (EXR), Lending Rate (LINTR) and Savings (SAV) in our model, explain approximately 97.75% of the variation of RGDP in Nigeria. It therefore goes without saying that other determinants of economic growth not captured in the model explain just 2.25% of the variation in RGDP in Nigeria.
   The adjusted R2 supports the claim of the R2 with a value of 0.975490 indicating that 97.55% of the total variation in the dependent variable, RGDP; jointly explained the independent variables.
   Durbin-Watson stat = 1.544971 shows the presence of autocorrelation.
3. The Durbin-Watson Statistics be corrected by (i) used of lagged values of the variables (ii) Re-specification of the mis-specified model (iii) including the omitted variables if any.

Descriptive Statistics Using Econometric software (E-Views)

## Table 1: Descriptive statistics

| Variable | Mean | Max. | Min. | Std. Dev. | Skew. | Kurt. | J-B | Prob. |
|---|---|---|---|---|---|---|---|---|
| GDPGR | 4.15 | 14.60 | -7.58 | 4.42 | -0.06 | 3.14 | 0.05 | 0.97 |
| UNEMPL | 8.90 | 19.70 | 1.80 | 4.97 | 0.50 | 2.31 | 2.36 | 0.31 |
| POV | 55.47 | 63.50 | 52.90 | 2.81 | 1.62 | 4.93 | 22.55 | 0.00 |
| PGR | 2.58 | 2.71 | 2.49 | 0.07 | 0.09 | 1.71 | 2.70 | 0.26 |

| | | | | | | | | |
|---|---|---|---|---|---|---|---|---|
| ADEPR | 89.08 | 92.76 | 86.62 | 2.02 | 0.53 | 1.87 | 3.83 | 0.15 |
| FERT | 6.15 | 6.78 | 5.17 | 0.41 | -0.19 | 2.36 | 0.87 | 0.65 |
| INEQ | 44.77 | 53.66 | 35.20 | 4.52 | -0.22 | 2.33 | 1.00 | 0.61 |
| LEXP | 48.10 | 53.99 | 45.64 | 2.85 | 0.92 | 2.28 | 6.16 | 0.05 |
| SSER | 38.75 | 54.17 | 23.92 | 10.24 | 0.16 | 1.62 | 3.18 | 0.20 |
| HEXP | 65.34 | 296.44 | 0.04 | 90.53 | 1.24 | 3.09 | 9.70 | 0.01 |

**Source: Author's computation from E-Views 9**

Descriptive statistics for the data used in the study are presented to highlight the pattern of distribution of the datasets. The annualized summary statistics of the data used in the empirical analysis are presented in Table 1. The Table shows the mean and other moment conditions for each of the variables. Average GDP growth rate was 4.15 percent over the study period, which indicates a relatively low growth rate of the economy since the 1980s. Considering that maximum value was 14.6 percent for the period, there is clear indication that the economy has not performed too well over a longer period of time in Nigeria. The minimum GDP growth rate is -7.58, suggesting that the economy has passed through many large swings in terms of both positive and negative growth rates. These large swings are confirmed by the high standard deviation which is relatively greater than the mean value. This indicates that there was a lot of variability in growth rates over the period, with certain periods having large declines and others having relatively high growth. This high variability of the growth rate of the economy presents certain difficulty in the manner of economic management and tools that can be used to achieve growth prospects over time. The population dynamics in the study could have contributed to the unsteady growth path of the Nigerian economy. The skewness values for GDP growth is however very low, which suggests that the mean value is largely representative of the performance of the growth rate over the entire period of the study. The J-B value of 0.05 is not significant at the 5 percent level which shows that the data series for economic growth is homogeneous for the years.

The other economic performance variables in the study are unemployment rate and poverty rate. The average unemployment rate in the study for the period is 8.9, which is very high, with a low standard deviation value of 4.97, suggesting that unemployment in Nigeria has been relatively high over the years. Proportion of individuals in poverty (living on less than 1.9 dollars a day) is 55.47 percent over the period. This also indicates a high poverty rate in the economy since 1980. Thus, with all the economic indicators combined (i.e., low growth rate of GDP, high poverty and unemployment rates), the Nigerian economic environment appears to be quite unstable and relatively weak.

Population growth rate is 2.57 percent is high on average over the period, with a maximum value of 2.71 and minimum value of 2.49. This shows that population growth rate has remained high for all the years and this high rate can be devastating for the economy, especially in years when growth rate of GDP was either low or negative. The other population indicators of fertility rate and adult dependency rate also indicate unhealthily large demographic indicators for Nigeria. Average fertility rate is 6.15, indicating that Nigerian women have up to 6 children on average. The dependency ratio of 89.08 is also high and shows that population in Nigeria puts a lot of pressure on the working class, which may intensify poverty and lower productivity. Average inequality of income is 44.77, while average life expectancy is 48.1 years for the Nigerian population over the years. Descriptive statistics using econometric package can be presented in charts as shown below.

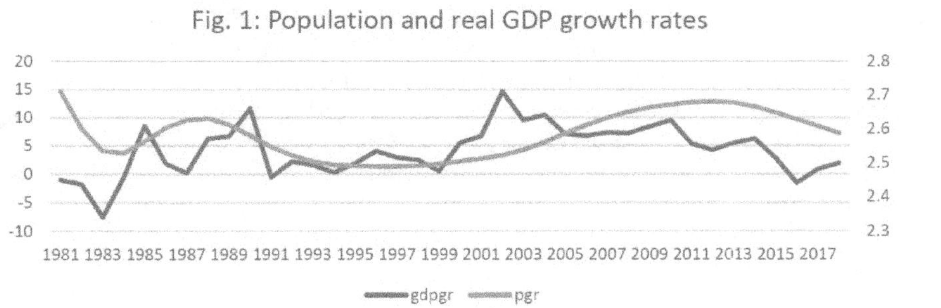


**Source: Author's computation from E-Views 9**

The trends in population and economic indicators in the economy are also presented in Charts above. Figure 1 shows the trend movement in economic growth and population growth for Nigeria over the years. Both rates appear to be moving in the same direction, especially when there are large swings in the business cycle. The poor performance has stagnated for long periods precisely because population growth has been so rapid in recent years.

## References

Adomgbor, F, C. (2002) *Introductory Economic Statistics* Delta, Miracle Publishers

Anyiwe, M.A. & Kelikume, I. (2006) *Applied Statistics in Social Sciences*, Benin City, Ethiope Publishing Corporation.

Asika, N. (2009) *Research Methodology in the Behavioural Sciences*, Ikeja, Longman Nigeria Plc

Gujarati, D.N, & Poter, D.C. (2009). *Basic econometrics*. 5th edition. Singapore: McGraw-Hill International Edition.

Gupta, S.C.(1984), Statistical Methods, New Delhi; Sultan Chand & Sons Publishers

Idele, S.I (1999) *Fundamentals of Economic Statistics*, Benin City, Goldband Publishers Int'l Ltd

Iyoha, M.A. (2004) *Applied Econometrics Revised Edition*, Benin City, Mindex Publishing.

Kabir, S.M.S. (2016). *Basic Guidelines for Research: An Introductory Approach for all Disciplines.* Book Zone Publication, ISBN: 978-984-33-9565-8, Chittagong-4203, Bangladesh.

Kabir, S.M.S. (2017). *Essentials of Counseling.* Abosar Prokashana Sangstha, ISBN: 978-984- 8798-22-5, Bangladazar, Dhaka-1100.

Kabir, S.M.S. & Rashid, U.K. (2017). Interpersonal Values, Inferiority Complex, and Psychological Well-Being of Teenage Students. *Jagannath University Journal of Life and Earth Sciences,* 3(1&2),127-135

Murray, R.S. (1972) *Statistics (S.I. Metric Edition):* Schaum's Outline Series. London: McGraw-Hill International Edition.

Obiojiofor, E.E. (1986) *Business Statistics:* Management Science Centre, University of Lagos, Lagos

Robert, L. (1977) *A Social Course in Statistics*, London, Cambridge University Press

# CHAPTER SEVEN

# TEST OF HYPOTHESES

**Sylvester Ohiomu**

## Introduction

A statistical hypothesis could be defined as statement or an assumption which may or may not be true concerning a sample or population. The term 'hypothesis' is an uncertain statement about the correlation between two or more variables. It is a testable and specific claim about what you expect to happen in your research. To be complete the hypothesis should contain three components namely:

- The variables;
- The population; and
- The relationship between the variables.

Hypothesis is distinct from both assumption (taking things for granted in order to simplify a model for logical procedure) and postulate (a statement assumed to be valid without a proof). A postulate states an assumption about some association between objects. It is the intended statement of an intention which the researcher seeks to substantiate or verify. It is an abridged simplification or generalization. This simplification requires information of principles or characteristics of things which relate to entire class of occurrences. The model when stated as a testable proposal formally and clearly and subjected to methodical or systematic verification is referred to as hypothesis. Remember, it predicts what the researchers intended in the goal of his or her research pending the outcome which may be right or wrong. Example "every good student in Mathematics is also good in Economics courses" which will be subject to further test of the belief with sample from a given population. Depending on the result obtained from the sample, you either accept the hypothesis or you discard the hypothesis. The hypothesis is a clear proclamation or proposition of what the research intends to investigate. It should be stated before commencement of the research and affirmed or disproved in reporting the results. Hypothesis allows to clarify: (1) the research objectives; (2) the concepts in the research; and (3) the relationship between the literature review and statement of problem.

A valid Hypothesis is conceptual in nature in a declarative form with empirical referent which is testable and verifiable construct. A good hypothesis plays significant role in empirical or socio-legal research. It not only navigates research in a proper direction but also contributes in testing or suggesting theories and describing a social or legal phenomenon. It is used to test theories, suggest new theories, describe social phenomena and suggest social policy.

## Importance of Hypotheses

Syed Mohammad Sajjad Kabir (2016) advocates the importance of hypothesis in the following ways:

- Hypotheses are necessary research instrument, for they build a link between the problem and the setting of empirical evidence in problem solving.
- A hypothesis provides the route that guides and accelerates the exploration of the phenomena under consideration.
- A hypothesis sport lights the problem. The investigator can examine thoroughly the factual and conceptual elements that appear to be related to a problem.
- Using hypothesis determines the relevancy of facts. A hypothesis directs the researcher's efforts into a productive channel.
- The hypothesis indicates not only what to look for is an investigation but how to obtain data. It helps in deciding research design. It may suggest what subjects, tests, tools, and techniques are needed.
- The hypothesis provides the researcher with the most efficient device or tool for discovering and clarifying the mysterious facts.
- A hypothesis offers the framework for drawing conclusions.

- These hypotheses simulate the investigator for further research studies.

## Characteristics of Hypotheses

A valid hypothesis must possess the following characteristics – (1) It is never formulated in the form of a question. (2) It should be empirically testable to determine its validity. (3) It should be definite, explicit or precise. (4) It should not contradict itself. (5) It should specify variables between which the relationship is to be established. (6) It should describe one issue only. A hypothesis can be formed either in descriptive or relational form. (7) It does not contradict existing laws

Research hypotheses are of different types: simple, complex, directional, non-directional, associative, causal, inductive & deductive, null, and alternative hypotheses. In Social Sciences, two main types of hypotheses namely Null and Alternative hypotheses are frequently used.

## Null (Ho) and Alternative ($H_1$) Hypotheses

The Null hypothesis is denoted with the symbol Ho it is formulated with an intention to reject, probably that there is no real difference between two values, if ever, the difference may be due to chance, that is to sampling error only. It states that there is no correlation between two constructs that the researcher compares on certain variables. Therefore, if you reject a null hypothesis, you inevitably accept an alternative hypothesis ($H_1$). The null hypothesis is always stated to specify the exact value of the population parameter while the alternative hypothesis is not. Examples, Ho: = 50 (the null hypothesis that the population mean equals 50

H1: < 50 or H1: >50

The Alternative hypothesis proposes a correlation between two or more variables, symbolized as H1.

## Formulating A Hypothesis

Before treating the concept of formulating a hypothesis, it is necessary to clarify the following sub titles frequently applied in testing a hypothesis. These include the following:

**Level of Significance:** The level of significance is the possibility of discarding a true null hypothesis that is the probability of "Type I error" and is denoted by α. The frequently used values of α are 0.05; 0.01; 0.1 etc. When, $\alpha = 0.05$ it means that level of significance is 5%. $\alpha = 0.01$ it means 1% level of significance. $\alpha = 0.01$ it means 10% level of significance. In fact, α specifies the critical region.

**Critical/ Rejection Region**: The critical region (CR) also called rejection region (RR) is the area within the curve beyond certain limits in which the population value is doubtful to fall by chance only when the null hypothesis is true. If an observed value falls in this region $H_0$ is rejected and the observed value is said to be significant. In a word, the region for which $H_0$ is rejected is called critical region

**Confidence Interval**: Confidence interval is the interval marked by limits within which the population value lies by chance and the hypothesis is considered to be tenable. If an observed value falls in confidence interval $H_0$ is accepted.

**Critical Values**: The values of the test statistic which separates critical region from confidence region (acceptance region) are called critical values.

**Standard Deviation**: The standard deviation is the most frequently calculated measure of variability or dispersion in a set of data points. The standard deviation value represents the average distance of a set of scores from the mean or average score. For example, if the average score on a test was 80 and the standard deviation was 2, the scores would be more clustered around the mean than if the standard deviation was 10. Where, SD = Standard Deviation; Σ = Sum of; X = Individual Score; M = Mean of All Scores; n = Sample Size (number of scores).

**Standard Error:** The standard error is an estimate of the standard deviation of a statistic. The standard error is important because it is used to compute other measures, like confidence intervals and margins of error. The standard error is computed from known sample statistics, and it provides an unbiased estimate of the standard deviation of the statistic.

**Degree of Freedom:** Degree of freedom (df) refers to the number of values which are free to vary after we have given the number of restrictions imposed upon the data. Thus in a 2x2 table, the degrees of freedom would be (2-1) (2-1) = 1 and in a 3x3 table, the df would be (3-1) (3-1) = 4.

## One – Tailed or Two – Tailed Tests:

A one tailed test is a test that restricts the significant level either to the extreme left or extreme right corner of the probability distribution curve.

For a two-tailed test, if the alternative hypothesis is that the population mean is not equal to 40, it means that such a parameter could be less than or more than 40. in this case, you divide the relevant significant level (α) in to equal parts, each appearing on the left extreme and right extreme of the probability distribution curve.

## Results of Hypothesis Testing:

Hypothesis testing enables a researcher to make decision about a population parameter by using a simple statistic. However, such decisions if not made properly are subject to possible errors like type 1 and type 11 error.

When a true hypothesis is accepted, a true decision has been made. When a false hypothesis is rejected, a correct decision has been taken.

## Type 1 and Type 11 Error

When a true hypothesis is rejected, an incorrect decision has been taken and this is called Type 1 error (alpha, α) ie Type 1 error óccurs if we reject the null hypothesis when it Is true.

When a false hypothesis is accepted, an incorrect decision has been taken and this is called type 11 error (beta, β) ie Type 11 error occurs when we the null hypothesis when it is false

| | Accept Ho | Reject Ho |
|---|---|---|
| Ho true | Correct decision | Type 1 error |
| Ho false | Type 11 error | Correct decision |

## Formal Procedure for Test of Significance

Step 1: Establish the Null hypothesis, Ho: U = X

Step 2: Establish the Alternative hypothesis, H1: U< X, H1: U> X

Step3: Select the level of significance (alpha) and the sample size

Step 4: Select appropriate test statistic and establish the critical area

Step 5: Compute the value of the statistic from a random sample of size n

Step 6: Accept or Reject the hypothesis accordingly at the level of significance selected. This implies that you state the statistical decision and the corresponding managerial conclusion using standard values from Distribution Tables.

**Exercises:** Example 1; Canada Homes Ventures Ltd introduced a new liquid detergent into the market with a mean cleansing capacity of 25 and a standard deviation of 0.5. Test the hypothesis that mean =25 against the alternative that mean is not equal to 25 if a random sample of 50 is tested and found to have a mean cleansing capacity of 24.4. (Assume 5% level of significance)

Solution; Given- Mean, $\overline{x} = 24.4$; Standard Deviation, SD = 0.5; n = 50

Step 1: Ho: $\mu = 25$

Step 2; H1: $\mu \neq 25$

Step3: $\alpha = 0.05$ (5%)

Step 4; Critical Region $Z < -1.96$ and $Z > 1.96$

Step 5; Computation

$$Z = (X - \mu) / {}^{\sigma}/_{\sqrt{n}}$$

By substitution

Z = 24.4 – 25/0.071

Z = -8.45

Step 6: Conclusion: we reject the Ho and conclude that the average cleansing capacity is not equal to 25 but less than it.

Example 2: In a Statistics Class a sample study of 64 students are obtained with mean 106, standard deviation 20, level of significance 0.05 and $H_0$: $\mu = 100$. Test the null hypothesis?

Solution: Given- Mean, $\overline{x}$ = 106; Standard Deviation, SD = 20; n = 64

Step 1: Null hypothesis, $H_0$: $\mu = 100$
Step 2; Alternative hypothesis, $H_1$: $\mu \neq 100$.
Step3: Level of significance, $\alpha = 0.05$ (0.5 – 0.025 = 0.4750)
Step 4; Critical Region Z < -1.96 and Z >1.96
Step 5; Computation

$$Z = (X - \mu)/ \sigma/\sqrt{n}$$

By substitution
Z = 106 – 100/2.5
Z = 2.4

Step 6: Conclusion: The obtained z -value 2.4 falls in the critical region (1.96), so the null hypothesis is rejected. Hence, we concluded that there is significant difference

## Statistical Power of Research

The power of a statistical test is the possibility that it correctly rejects the null hypothesis when the null hypothesis is incorrect. If the power increases, the chances of a Type II error occurring decrease. The probability of a Type II error occurring is referred to as the false negative rate (β) and the power is equal to 1− β. The power is also known as the sensitivity.

## Power of a Test

| Decision on Null Hypothesis | Null Hypothesis True | Null Hypothesis False |
|---|---|---|
| Accept | Correct Decision Probability = 1- α (Confidence Level) | Type 11 Error Probability = β |
| Reject | Type I error Probability = α α is called significance level | Correct Decision Probability =1− β 1− β is called Power of a test |

There are many factors that affect the power of a test, the probability of rejecting $H_0$ when it is false. These include:

1. Discrepancy Between the True Population Mean (μt) and the Hypothesized Mean (μh): The larger the discrepancy, the greater the power.
2. Sample Size: The larger the size of the sample, the smaller the standard error of the mean and the greater the power of the test.
3. Standard Deviation of the Variable: The smaller the standard deviation, the greater the power. The standard deviation can be reduced by improving the reliability of the measuring instrument.
4. Relation Between the Samples (More than one Mean): Dependent samples can increase power. In general, the higher the correlation induced by pairing, the stronger the effect on power.
5. Level of Significance: The larger the value of $\alpha$, the lower the value of $\beta$ and the greater the power.
6. Choice of $H_1$: Power is greater for a one-tailed test than for a two-tailed test (when the direction specified by H 1 is correct).

## Criteria for Evaluating Hypothesis

Some hypotheses are considered more satisfactory than others. The following are the various considerations of a satisfactory hypothesis and these criteria may be helpful to make this judgement.

Plausibility of Explanation: A valid hypothesis should have relevant and logical possibility about the correlation of variables.

Testability of Explanation: The variables should be defined operationally and the predicted relations among them can be tested empirically. The variables of the hypothesis should be measurable or quantifiable. The suitable measuring instrument is available or it can be considered easily.

Adequacy of Scope: The most useful hypotheses explain all the facts that are relevant to the phenomena being explained and contradict none of them. The broader the scope of a theory, the more valuable it is. The more consequences that a hypothesis yields, the greater is its fruitfulness. A hypothesis is of greater value if it establishes a generalization that can be applied in many areas of education or in many fields. The most satisfactory hypotheses not only explain all the known facts that gave rise to the original problems but also enable scientists to make predictions about as yet unobserved events and relationships.

Usefulness of False Hypotheses: Hypotheses need not be the correct answers to problems to be useful. In almost every inquiry a scholar formulates several hypotheses and hopes that one will provide a satisfactory solution to the problem. By eliminating the false hypotheses one by one the investigator keeps narrowing the field in which the answer must lie. The testing of false hypotheses is also of value if it directs the attention of scientists to unsuspected facts or relations they eventually help in solving the problem.

Roots in Existing Theories: A useful educational hypothesis, therefore, adds something to previously established knowledge by supporting, qualifying, refuting or enlarging upon existing theories. A hypothesis that is compatible with well attested theories is in a favourable position to advance

Hence, the basic criteria for evaluating research hypotheses are – (a) stated in declarative form; (b) consistent with known facts, prior research, or theory; (c) logical extension of the research problem; (d) states an expected relationship between two or more variables; (e) can be tested; and (f) is clear and concise.

## References


Adomgbor, F, C. (2002) *Introductory Economic Statistics* Delta, Miracle Publishers

Anyiwe, M.A. & Kelikume, I. (2006) *Applied Statistics in Social Sciences*, Benin City, Ethiope Publishing Corporation.

Asika, N. (2009) *Research Methodology in the Behavioural Sciences*, Ikeja, Longman Nigeria Plc

Gujarati, D.N, & Poter, D.C. (2009). *Basic econometrics*. 5th edition. Singapore: McGraw-Hill International Edition.

Idele, S.I (1999) *Fundamentals of Economic Statistics*, Benin City, Goldband Publishers Int'l Ltd

Iyoha, M.A. (2004) *Applied Econometrics Revised Edition*, Benin City, Mindex Publishing.

Kabir, S.M.S. (2016). *Basic Guidelines for Research: An Introductory Approach for all Disciplines.* Book Zone Publication, ISBN: 978-984-33-9565-8, Chittagong-4203, Bangladesh.

Kabir, S.M.S. (2017). *Essentials of Counseling.* Abosar Prokashana Sangstha, ISBN: 978-984- 8798-22-5, Bangladazar, Dhaka-1100.

Kabir, S.M.S. & Rashid, U.K. (2017). Interpersonal Values, Inferiority Complex, and Psychological

Well-Being of Teenage Students. *Jagannath University Journal of Life and Earth Sciences,* 3(1&2),127-135

Murray, R.S. (1972) *Statistics (S.I. Metric Edition):* Schaum's Outline Series. London: McGraw-Hill International Edition.

Obiojiofor, E.E. (1986) *Business Statistics:* Management Science Centre, University of Lagos, Lagos

Robert, L. (1977) *A Social Course in Statistics*, London, Cambridge University Press

# CHAPTER EIGHT

# THE RELEVANCE OF HISTORY IN SOCIAL AND LEGAL RESEARCH

**Harriet Omokiniovo Efanodor-Obeten and Anthony Iyoha Emhenya**

## Introduction

Attempt has been made to establish the dichotomy between history, social and legal studies, in terms of their methodology, scope and subject matter. Similarly, there is already a large body of literature on the nature and methods of history. Many of these studies raise difficult epistemological questions about the nature of historical evidence and research. Unfortunately, studies have not seriously examined the role of historical thinking and materials outside the discipline of history as such, much emphasizes has not been placed on the relevance of history to social and legal research. The distinction between history, social and legal research, has its origin in the controversy which centres around methodology rather than on methods. Bailey (1982:29) defined method as the research technique or tool used to gather data, while methodology is the philosophy of the research process, which includes the assumptions and values that serve as a rationale for research and the standards or criteria, the researcher uses for investigating data and reaching conclusions.

Broadly defined, research is the process of identifying a problem and finding solutions to the problem. Research process is a complex one which involves many things such as, problem identification, theory/concept application, literature review, interpersonal communications and data analysis (Oyibo, 1992:19). Research therefore is a reflective seeking or intensive search with a view to becoming certain. In this regard certain research methods or methodologies are used in carrying out research. Ofo (1994:1) explained that the choice of which research method to be used in any investigation depends on the purpose of the study and the type or nature of the problem to be investigated.

However, there are some branch of knowledge which in their methods of investigation as well as in the knowledge they impact, are so closely allied, that no one who would stand high in that profession can afford to neglect them (Aydelotte, 1966). Foremost among these stands history.

History has a base in both social and legal studies. History like social sciences and law alike deal with the affairs of men. Social scientist and legal practitioners deal with the ever-changing life of man in his environment which could dates back to centuries, hence in order to understand man in the present, there is a need to rely on an approach that deals with the chronological account of event.

As a consequence, over the past decades, an increasing number of social and legal studies have been developing the practice of adopting what is known as the historical social and legal research. Economist, political scientist, sociologist and law practitioners are increasingly working with historical evidence. Adopting historical social and legal research involved a process of borrowing concepts, methods and techniques from history. It also entails systematic analysis to understand the social and legal order and its long run changes over time.

The objective of this chapter is to bring to the fore, the relevance of history to social and legal research. The reason is based on the fact that in recent times there are substantive advancement in the manner in which social and legal research think about the past. It could be said that lately, history has proven useful as one of the wide range of alternative methodologies or approaches for understanding social phenomena. The interaction between history, social and legal studies has far more to offer. It provides opportunities for conceptual reconstruction and for theory development. The significance of historical social and legal research lies in its impact on the traditional way in which history has been constructed, taught about and written about for many decade, and which in text after text, remain relatively unchanged.

## Understanding History And Historical Research

History as a body of knowledge about the past especially the past acts of man in society and consists of facts attained through honest inquiry and generalization arrived at by historian. History is the study of what man has done in his social capacity in the past which is used to explain the present and project into the future.

Research in the writing of history deals with the determination, evaluation and explanation of the past event essentially for the purpose of gaining a better and clearer understanding of the present and making a more reliable prediction of the future. It involves critical and objective methods of inquiry with generalisations made from organized knowledge. Its distinctive features includes the use of qualitative, critical analytical method and interpretation of findings (Obasi 1999:61).

### Generalisation in the writing of History

As the line between history and other social sciences becomes increasingly distinct. Historians agree for the most part on two major fact that (1) historical writings inevitably contains generalisations, but historians do not usually make them explicit. (2) Generalizations are used because, at the least, events must be selected for study, terms must be used to portray them, and account must order details in meaningful sequences (Hopkins 1964:635). The scientist makes the formulation of general laws or generalization its major preoccupation. Scientist generalize about certain occurrences in the course of their studies hence there are many laws. In other words, the scientist regards the frequent formulations of such laws as revolutions of scientific study. The social scientist also preoccupy themselves with the formulations of law. For example in political science, there is the law which states that "power corrupt but absolute power corrupt absolutely." The natural science and social science as well make the formulation of laws the focus of their research but the historians does not make the formulation of law as the focus or main preoccupation of his research (Odafe 2003). But it must be quickly pointed out that historians even though does not make the formulation of laws his preoccupation or major focus, in his study none the less generalization is indispensable in historical explanation. The concept of a period is impossible without employing an implicit generalization that some at least of the human experiences encountered with a given time span have more in common with each other than with earlier or later event (Partington, 1980). Periodization is among what Finlay term classification and Wright label generalization. Almost every useful noun or adjectives used in historical explanation contains or implies a theoretical judgment about general characteristics (Partington, 1980). Han Meyeroff (cited in Partington) has challenged the definition of classification and labelling generalisations as true generalization and suggested that they are classification or abstract concepts or ideal types more simply they are abbreviations or shorthand description. Thus objection may not carry, much conviction since to describe them as classification, abstract concept or Weberian ideal types does not make them any less generalization. Partington (1980) further drew attention to the generalization implicit in terms such as slave, feudal, medieval, modernization, and imperialism. Historians seek to explain their content and significance and the changes and the continuities within them, in specific historical context. The most important problem historian face in historical generalization is that of generic characteristics.

Porter (1963) is clearly on the side of those who want a more rigorous use of theoretical generalization in historical writing. The historian really cannot abstain from generalization and cannot escape theory. The choice before him is not between a factual and a theoretical approach but between, on the one hand, theoretical assumptions which have been recognized and so far as possible, made rational and explicit and, on the other, unrecognized, half-hidden assumptions which unordered and chaotic.

Gotteschalk (1963) distinguishes kinds of historian according to the level of generalization they customarily employ. The first consist of those who make generalization only if they were unaware that they are doing so and try to eliminate the ones of which they unaware. The second kind are those who propound philosophies that are intended to provide cosmic understanding of the course of human events, past and to come. In between comes those who make highly limited generalization, those who generalize to specific other times of places; and those who generalize to indefinite times or places.

## Uniqueness in the writing history

History remember the conscious of what happened in a particular occasion. It is not about what usually happen under circumstances. History is about what actually happened at a clearly specified period of time in all detail and in the context of what preceded it. The historian concentrate on one event in its unique individuality not as and instead of a type not as a member of a class but as something which is to be viewed for and himself and his interest in event for and in themselves is regarded as a distinguishing feature of historical right. Uniqueness is regarded as a quality which historical event possess any attempt to subdue them under a general law or to assimilate them to other event of similar kind is to go against the nature of historical facts (Nowell-Smith (1957).

## Sources of historical formation

The term sources here is used for the tangible and intangible things that yield historical information, if studied with the professional skill of the historian. There are three kind of sources in history. (a) oral tradition like eye-witness accounts, and participants or historical objects that can be examined and (b) secondary sources such as information recorded by another person or events observed by such person, data from books, newspapers, periodicals or archival records written by others (Obasi 1999:61) (c) archeological evidence and artifact or historical object that can be examined. The different types of sources are completely not mutually exclusive. Written sources can be complemented with oral sources. When historian want to go very far back, the written and oral sources are not sufficient to answer the questions which the historian will ask, he must necessarily resort to archaeological evidence. The importance of sources of history cannot be over emphaised after deciding what topic to investigate the historians has to identify the sources that are most likely to yield evidence on his work. This sources provide the historian with the raw materials with which to make his real structure of the past.

## Statement in the writing of history

In order to understand the value of the different types of sources, it is absolutely necessary to grasp, the meaning of three kinds of statement in terms of which the nature and significance of each of the main inquires of sources are described and they are; statement of fact; statement of inferences and statement of opinion.

Facts: a fact is a statement that is commonly accepted as the truth in itself and of itself and need no other addition or qualification to make it true. Historical facts are words that are commonly accepted as true among historians. However, unlike facts in science and other empirical studies, they are not provable in laboratories. For instance that the Nigerian civil war broke out in May 1967 and ended in January 1970 is a statement of fact. That Abraham Lincoln was assassinated in April 1865 is a fact. Facts of this kind may not depend on any form of judgment. However, there are other facts that are commonly regarded as facts simply because they are generally accepted by historians and their status as fact is established through the careful judgment of the historian. The significance of the fact which must be recognized is that they are as Conton and Schneider put it, the foundation stories for further thinking about history without fact, there can be no history (Odafe, 2003).

## Inferences in history

Historian see the relations among the facts on the basis of the facts. They build a more subjective and less dependable category of statements called inferences. The inference are statements that emerges from carefully observed and true relationship among facts. The professional judgment of the historian is indispensable on the creation of inferences. If two or more historians are given a few sources of facts and they begin to work with them, the relationship they observe is the inferences they make which may not be the same in all respects but most of the possible relationship they can see among the fact given and the inferences will tend to be similar bearing in mind the similarity in the professional training of the historians and the impersonal nature of the fact.

The truth of an inference depends on the extent to which the information it is based on is true, that is based on the facts. It is not enough to base the inference on just any member of facts. It is necessary to take all the facts available into account while the nature of a fact does not change even if new facts are added to the set to which it belongs. The nature of the inference can be changed with the addition of one new fact. The reliability of an inference increase with the number of facts on which it is based. The status of inference in history is such that they need to be re-examined constantly because new facts about matter of which histories had be written come to light on any given time than new facts in the sciences. The fact that they came in great numbers makes each of them less easily noticeable than in the case of the sciences where each new facts is easily noticed that it is described as revolutionary in history. Since new facts came to light almost every day owing to the nature of historical inquiry, it is essential to examine existing inferences to ensure that they conform to the latest facts available. The process of re-examination is therefore a never ending process (Odafe, 2003).

Opinion: the third find of statement historian deal with is opinion. Opinions can be defined as personal and individual conclusion, identical in kind to inference but without any support or grounding in facts. They usually arise from the historian prejudices or acceptance of other people's opinion which have been confused with fact. The confusion of inference and opinion fact is a common sources of error in history writing.

## Understanding Social and Legal Research

### Social Research

Social research can be defined as the systematic and objective analysis and recording of controlled observation that may lead to the development of generalization, principles or theories resulting in prediction and possible control of events in society. It attempts to answer or solve social problems. Social research is interdisciplinary in nature. Social research can be described as either basic or applied. Basic research is a fact finding research that explores the situation or phenomenon in order to learn about it and answer any question or questions relating to it. The attention of the researcher here is focused on the question. While applied research explains or exposes a situation in order to enable the researcher understand it better, hence it is often called explanatory research or expository research. Applied research is aimed at discovering why certain events, situations or phenomena occur. It answers the question why because of the orientation of the question it attempts to answer, explanatory research assumes that the problem of investigation exist or has been properly established to have occurred (Asika 2008:12-13).

Social research are concerned with the analysis of human behavior. To analyse human behavior, they all follow a common trend, which is developing and using systematic, causal relationships of behavior form the cornerstone of any social research. Explanations about human behavior are offered and they are conventionally referred to as models since they provide mere statements about the most important determinants of the behaviour being investigated. In social research, models by design, represents simplifications and abstractions of reality and they help to describe the most important systematic aspects of behavior seen in a wide variety of circumstance, rather than completely according for specific events (Gbadesyesin and Oyeranti, 2005). Unlike the natural and physical sciences, where there is a dominant methodological tradition, the situation is different in the social sciences where there are competing epistemologies which in turn give rise to competing methodological traditions. In social research methodology can be classified into quantitative and qualitative research. The classification also reflect the two methodological schools or tradition which are traditional and behaviourial schools. The traditionalist are more historical, normative, and descriptive as well as largely qualitative. They try to interpret social actions in order to enhance understanding by applying logic. Thus social phenomena are understood through direct observation, communication with participants, or analysis of text (Obasi 1999:17). The behaviouralist on the other hand, apply the positivistic method which emphaises the application of the scientific method to the study of social phenomena. They lay emphasis on observation, verification and measurement. The behaviouralist are more analytical quantitative and theory building conscious (Obasi 1999:17).

Social research consist of series of steps necessary to efficiently carryout research on any social phenomena. These are;

1. Sensing or realizing problem: this involves observing the situation and sensing problem as new problems keep on emerging in the social environment.

2. Problem identification: once one become aware of what is happening in the environment, he/she would than focus on the problem .i.e. identify what exactly are the problems in the situation.
3. Theoretical framework: once the problem is identified, the researcher carefully studies the earlier studies. This help to integrate information for the problem to be conceptualized. This help to develop theoretical framework.
4. Hypothesis formulation: a hypothesis is a tentative answer to question. It is subjected to the process of verification or disconfirmation.
5. Research design: it is a plan, structure and strategy for conducting research. It describes the general framework for collecting analyzing and evaluating data.
6. Collection of data: at this stage, the researcher has to collect data as expected. Data can be obtained from primary and secondary sources. Questionnaire, interview and observation are major instrument to collect data.
7. Data analysis: it is the statistical analysis of data that has been collected, edited, coded and tabulated.
8. Interpretation and generalisation: this takes the result of data analysis makes inference pertinent to the research relation studied and draw conclusion about relations. Generalisation is the act of giving general form to these conclusions.
9. Report presentation: finally the researcher prepare the report.(www.jaram.com.ppl)

## Legal Research

The nature of legal studies is such that it touches the practical life of man at every point in his relations with his social environment. Legal studies as be described as a process of identifying and retrieving information necessary to support legal decision making. Legal research may be defined as the systematic investigation towards increasing the sum knowledge of law. It involves ascertaining what the law is on an identified topic or in the given area as well as the enquiry into law with the view to expanding the science of law (Chegwe 2016).

Laws are made to regulate man's activities in the society. Commenting on the relationship between law and society, Gasiokwu (1994) has this to say,

> *"the relationships between the different strata of society are regulated by a body of rules commonly referred to as law, so that law could therefore be referred to as an instrument both of social control and of social change. The attitude of members of the society towards legal precepts or legal institutions is dictated by the relationships which the law sets out to establish or regulate at any particular time or place. This in turn is determined primarily by the class interest of the law maker. The law which regulates all aspects of our social life are made by men for men, and are operated, implemented and enforced by human beings through various legal institutions. The status of such institutions, the effect of particular laws, or the sentiments of the people, or the operation of certain legal machinery, may also become the subject matter of legal research."*

Law influences social values and code. Societal values and norms also influence law directly or indirectly as it tries to mould and control these values, attitudes and behavioural pattern so that they flow in a proper channel. As it attempts either to support the social system or to change the prevalent social situations or relationships, by its former process of rules and sanctions, law also influences other parts of the social system. The societal values and patterns as can be observed are dynamic and complex, and this dynamism of societal values make the discipline of law dynamic and complex. Such a complex nature of law and its application requires systematic approach to the understanding of law and its operational dynamics. A systematic investigation into these aspects of law helps in knowing the existing and emerging legislative policies, laws, their social relevance and efficacy. Legal research therefore involves a process of identifying and retrieving information necessary to support decision making (Khushal and Philipus (2009).

There are two main broad categories of legal research. These are Non-doctrinal legal research and Doctrinal Research. They are obviously not mutually exclusive since they overlap. Doctrinal research is the research into doctrines. It involves analysis of case law and statutory provisions by application of the power of reasoning. The main characteristics of doctrinal research according to Gasiokwu (1994) are;

1. The scholar organises his study around legal prepositions, and

2. Primary sources are the main source of data, secondary sources play only supportive roles

Doctrinal research is the research into law as a normative science, that is the science which lays down norms and standards for human behaviour in a specified situation or situations enforceable through the sanctions of s State. It is this normative character that distinguishes law from other related discipline of other social sciences. Doctrinal research is a research into law as it stands in the books, it is speculative in nature. Speculative in the sense that it consists in pondering over the essence and main qualities of law. The various viewpoints which are admissible within it cannot be compared because they cannot be empirically verified. Another name for doctrinal research is research into theory. It involves an enquiry into conceptual basis of legal rules, principles or doctrine. It provides stimulus and intellectual infrastructure for empirical research though it is not empirical (Gasiokwu 1994).

Non-doctrinal research is the research of the actual working of the law in society in relation with other interdependent factors. It researches the relationship between law and other behavioural sciences. Here the emphasis is not really on legal doctrines and concepts but on people, social values and social institutions. Non-doctrinal research takes either some aspects of the legal decision process, or the people and institutions supposedly regulated by law as the focus of study. In non-doctrinal research, data needed to answer questions are not ordinarily available in conventional legal sources. Hence field work is usually required for this type of research. Most non-doctrinal research may seek:

1. To assess the impact of non-legal events e.g. economic development, growth of knowledge, technical changes upon legal decision processes.
2. To identify and appraise the magnitude of variable factors influencing the outcome of legal decision making e.g., the effect of capital punishment on the prevalence of dangerous crime at a given place at a given time.
3. To trace the consequences of the outcome or legal decision making in terms of values, gains and deprivation of litigants, non-litigants and non-legal institutions.

From the above, the historians, social scientist and legal practitioners alike deal with the affairs of men, the most uncertain of all subjects of investigation. Therefore numerous topics and problems will draw from each other. The next section will examine the relevance of history to social and legal research.

## Relevance of History to Social and Legal Research

History by its definition and practices embraces aspect of social and legal studies as they contribute to its proper understanding. Since man has adapted his life to his physical and social environment, every discipline dealing with the mental, spiritual, social and physical aspects of human development must be relevant to history. This does not however, imply that all other disciplines are subsidiary to history. Rather it suggest the essential unity of real knowledge especially when such knowledge relates to the study of man, further it means that just as other discipline are required for a full and satisfactory historical understanding, therefore, history constitute an important ingredient for other humanistic and social research.

The study of history includes a survey of man's economic, religious, intellectual, legal and social developments as well as the study of states, their growth and organization and their relationship with one another. History is the principal traditional approach dealing with chronological account of events. Historical records are very useful in the study of social and legal phenomena. Social and legal researcher therefore selects facts from history and uses historical method in some aspects of their social and legal analysis. Thus, the study and understanding of history is important in social and legal research as it serve as a guide and it reveals certain aspects of the stages of development of man and societies from the past to the present. It helps social and legal research focusing on the extent to which the practice of a nation has conformed to norms, law and goals, to trace the courses of different policies, programmes, events and responses in their historical context. The views and precedents of the past helps the researcher to discover how decisions were reached by looking at the inputs and outputs in the decision making process over time. Besides actions of men in their social environment can be best understood by making references to history.

Social and legal research involves the use of techniques as well as concept and methods. Considerable, there is a growing amount of social and legal research which now think about the past. Therefore as a consequence, the social and legal research involves the use of new concepts, different ways of defining problems, and different contexts in which to ask research questions. Such research seek to describe pattern within the social order both at one time and as it changes over a long period of time. There is the masses of historical evidence which bear on social and legal research, and which if put together intuitively for descriptive purposes, have often generated accurate description. Thus history provides the technique, concepts and methods needed for the growing amount of the historical social and legal research which think about the past. Historical questions are defined in these research not only in terms of the outcome of particular events, but also the patterns of event, ideas, perceptions and actions, and especially long development in those pattern (Hays 1974). For example, one is no longer concerned mainly with economic outcomes of civil war, as an isolated event, but with the role they played in long run trends of economic growth and development over time. Similarly, elections are thought of not in terms of single happenings but in terms of the role they played in long run patterns of electoral behavior.

Also social and legal studies also rely on some form of quantitative historical records. The use of quantitative method in history increased dramatically in the 1960's and declined sharply after the Mid-1980's (Ruggles and Magnusm 2019). However, lately, with changing character of historical evidence, the growing body of research by non-historian into historical problems and the increasing surge in historical social research, there is the increased use of systematic analysis, theory and quantification in historical research and writing (SSRC, 2016). The above has resulted in enormous quantitative historical records. Quantification in history is a way of improving the customary undertakings and objectives of historical facts and evidence. For instance, historical studies of the slave trade have included statistical element in an attempt to estimate the total number of Africans taken over to America or the effect of such population movement on the growth of population and historical development in Africa. As such Katz (2013) described history as one, which when its outcome, when properly pursued, will be valid generalization which contribute to both contemporary social theory and practice. Quantitative historical records of trade sometimes take the form of lists of quantities of the numbers of copies made, distributed, and sold. This is usually patchy, but the data can provide insight into the production and consumption since earliest times. The above can be useful in the detection of historical trends and significant variables in pattern of trade, migration and development of societies. It can weigh the potential of geographical mapping for the histories of trade development and capable for big data analysis of the digitized text to propose computational models for social and legal research (Weedon, 2019).

Social and legal research which also think about the past also entails systematic analysis to understand the social order and its long run changes. History also provide the researcher with the skills and techniques to find evidence and analyse these evidences accurately. For instances, as legal studies gathers facts from the uncertain memories of living witnesses, as the study draws his principles from the contradictory statements contained in books, the researcher then like the historian, must cross-examine his authors, probe their motives, estimate the influence of their prejudicary, balance their testimony against that of the others and finally determine, by a preponderance of proof, the point at issue. The historical techniques provide the social and legal researcher on how to find evidence for himself. When social and legal studies researcher enters into the broader domain of international law. They must rely wholly upon history for precedents. Here, there is no supreme power to prescribe rules of action, no supreme court with jurisdiction to decide or power to enforce its decree. Thus the law by which a state are to be judged, in or in peace, are to be learned only from the public history of the nations and the history of the intercourse of one nation with another is so intimately connected with the internal history of each that no one can understand the former without some knowledge of the latter (Wilson, 1887).

The historical approach is also important in the comprehension of statutory laws used for legal research. A legal researcher who hopes to comprehend any law without studying their background is setting himself an impossible task. The above is so because, first, very few pieces of legislation are original in the sense of being pre innovations of a skilled draftsman. In the majority of cases, the researcher need to consults and adapts earlier statutes or make use of principles laid down or proposed in decided cases over time. Secondly, laws are not made in a vacuum. They are passed in order to meet some needs of society, while they may not always reflect the true wishes of the people, or even of the ruling group, they reflect nevertheless, the historical and political spirit of the day (Ellinger and Keith 2015).

Social and legal research involves a distinctive method which is systematic rather than intuitive. There is a self-conscious attempt to hold in balance a conceptual framework derived from whatever source, general social theory, the implications of specific studies, contemporary analysis and historical evidence. There is the constant interaction between testing alternative theories with alternative bodies of oral evidences, and modifying thereby with the more precise description of historical relationships. Historical description help to sharpen distinctions with clear cut alternatives. It is important to place problems in a comparative context so that more than one instance of a phenomenon can be dealt with and the general can be sorted out from the particular. From one point of view, this merely enriches the use of historical description by making more precise and differentiated from another, it enables one to test alternative descriptions and hypotheses (Hays, 1974).

Some understanding of historical event is an essential part of civic knowledge and awareness for any researcher and a greater appreciation of historical development can particularly enrich researcher's work, both by opening new avenues of research and also by offering a deeper understanding of the work that social and legal researcher do. Social and legal development cannot be separated from other historical trends then a sense of history is vital to understanding the society and law. Areas that provides such vital understanding of history are the legal and social history. It is therefore pertinent to ask, does social and legal history matters or why is it important to have an historical approach to law and social research? In some respect, of course, the answer to the question of why social and legal history matters is the same as the answer to the question of why history of any kind matters. That is, it is always better to understand not just the shape that some aspect of our present world takes, but also how it got that way. Moreover, our history is more than an explanation of past developments. It is an essential form of understanding of the world around us, because it is invariably still with us, aspect of it remain embedded in every part of our society. Thus we shall explore first, why legal history and then, social history matters in legal and social research.

There are principal reasons why legal history matters to researchers. Legal history matters because it provides the researcher with facts about contingency of law, about its fundamental shaping by other historical forces, about facts that law is not a set of abstract, ahistorical and universal principles, it does not exist in a vacuum. Rather, it is formed by, and exists within, human societies, and its forms and principles, and changes to them, are rationally connected to those particular societies. For instance, within the realm of common law doctrine, Morton's Horwitz's (1977) book, "The transformation of American Law, 1780-1860" is a case in point, Horwitz made use of legal history to locate the transformation of American law within the context of historical change. Horwitz argued that the changing economy and new political ideas of the late eighteenth and nineteenth centuries were responsible for substantial alterations to many common law doctrines, alternatives which benefitted the new commercial and industrial classes at the expense of farmers and artisan. He also showed that this occurred through what he termed an "instrumentalist style of judicial reasoning" (Horwitz 1977). One which openly and self-consciously adapted doctrine to circumstance and to changing ideologies, especially the rise of free market principles (Philips 2010; Smith and Mclaren 2001). Thus, Horwitz's book demonstrate to the legal researcher, the idea of how one can and should locate change in actual material circumstances, changing ideologies and historical context.

Another reason why legal history matters for understanding the complexity of law is that it allows the researcher to see what we think of as the law today, and then assume to have always been the case, has in fact not always predominated. This understanding is not just about the practices of the institution but also brings to the fore that the ideas underlying those practices were radically different from what they are today. Like all history, legal history produces winners and losers. Loser are those vision of society and belief systems lost out in the struggle with other visions. Legal history enables us to excavate the past from such phenomena to show that there have been, and thus are, arguably legitimately different ways to think about many things, including legal orders. A researcher who study is devoted to understanding of alternatives that have actually become the norm after a period of being lost can rely on legal history. Philips (2010) gave an excellent illustration of the role of history in the modern development of the law relating to aboriginal rights in Canada. According to Philips (2010), in a famous statement in 1969 then Canadian Prime Minister Pierre Trudeau announced that there was no such thing as rights for aboriginal people distinct from those held by all other Canadians. In a sense he was right, for one could not find any judicial or legislative statement to the contrary in the twentieth century. But those few legal historians who had looked at the question had found a variety of sources, some cases and also government policies, some dealing with areas that became part of Canada, others dealing with other parts of the empire that said differently, that said that at one time it was part of the common law that indigenous peoples had rights in their land and other kinds of rights. But that legal tradition that had been effectively erased from the law books and thus from the world view of society and politicians. Indeed in Canada it was so much lost that in 1927 it was made an offence to raise money for the purpose of prosecuting Indian land claims without the consent of the superintendent general of Indians. When the matter did finally get into a courtroom, and to the Supreme Court of Canada in the *Calder* case in the early 1970s, the Court relied on cases and practices long forgotten to assert, or rather re-assert, the idea of native title (Philips 2010).

Therefore, the role that legal history can play in exposing the degree of legal pluralism in our system, past and present, is by no means restricted to ideas that were once the mainstream, became forgotten, and have now been revived. Legal pluralism appears in many other guises historically, and these may well have a contemporary co-existence with other legal orders. Studying the past, will enables the researcher to chart the co-existence with state based laws.

Social history also matters to researchers. Social history refers to a sub discipline of the historical science on one hand and to a general approach to history that focuses on society at large on the other hand. Social historians sought to uncover the relationship between economics, demographic and social processes and structures as well as their impact on social stratification, political institutions, social movements, ideologies and forms of public and private behaviours (Conrad, 2015). Researcher's use of historical approaches in the social sciences basically proceed within a generalizing from a reference. For instance historical economics follows the basic ideas of uncovering time/space bound economic laws and regularities. Also historical sociology is primarily oriented to the general features of time/space bound social processes, patterns, and figuration. In parallel, historical approaches in the political sciences concentrate on general features of political development. Also historicized versions of anthropology are interested in the general evolutionary patterns of human behavior (Spohn 2015).

History consist of changes which social structures undergo. Each change, is containing within itself all its past and seed of its future. Smelser's (1959) study entitled social change in the industrial revolution testifies in unmistakable terms, to how well historical data may be employed by a researcher interested in testing the general propositions about the process of long-term social changes, Smelser uses a great deal of data from the industrial and social history of Lancashire covering a period of over seventy years commencing from 1770, with a view to providing an empirical test of general theory of change in social systems through process of structural differentiation. Smelser utilized the data of history as a useful type of material to inject content into his trans-historic theoretical scaffold. The theory is a part of the wider theory of social action developed by Talcott Parsons (Desai ND).

Obviously, any developmental approaches cannot do without historical materials. When one speaks of a change from primitive society to a modern society or from the informal to formal organisation of production or business, is usually in effect, the conceptions which derives their validity from historical study. The comparative method, draws its breath from history, the approach consists in comparison being drawn between different societies with the view of explaining the variation in social structure and culture. Such comparison involves or must involve, in principle, the societies of the past as well as of the present. The exponent of comparative method cannot afford to neglect the vast information about man and society which the past has to offer, regardless of what materials are available about the contemporary societies.

The 1960's and thereafter has been characterized by profound political, economic and social changes, crises and violence. With the pre-occupation and obsession with methods and techniques by social scientist rather than focusing on substance in social research resulted often result in the neglect of some aspects of social research. There are aspect of social research that are not readily subject to measurement. Thus the search for relevance or the meaningful application of social and political knowledge to socio-political issues of the day has drawn upon the historical method by providing answers. History is relevant to social and legal research because it has variety of sources that can be used to explain aspects of social research that cannot be subject to measurement and those tradition that had been effectively erased from the books and thus from the world view of society. For instance Experience as an historical source of knowledge is not only valuable in the research enterprise but actually facilitate the acquisition knowledge. Experience provides researchers with raw materials not only to develop research questions but also devise research strategies to actualize their research objective. Oral tradition is useful to recall traditions that have been erased from the book because knowledge generated through tradition is often passed from generation to generation through cultural mechanism such as family, folklores and other media, and religious institutions.

In summation, numerous research topics and modern problems of social and legal research draw heavily from history. Such topics and problems which border around issues of immigration, foreign trade, world resources, and development of modern states, international law, transportation, communication and international relation cannot be research into without extensive use of historical records, techniques and methods.

## Conclusion

There are various methods of seeking knowledge. These methods which at times compete are also complementary. Historians, social scientist and legal practitioner alike deal with the affairs of men. History is concerned, not with mere events, but with human actions. Social and legal research are based on logic and empirical observation. It involves the interaction between ideas and evidence, and evidence help to extend, revise and test ideas. In dealing with the ever changing world social and legal research would rely on historical evidence and facts. History provide evidence, serves as a guide and reveals certain aspects of the stages of development of man and societies from the past to the present. History has always been a lender. The field of social sciences and law are not a self-contained field of study, whose boundaries do not transverse into history. The study of man in his environment is a continuum and history is a bridge between social sciences and humanities.

## References

Asika N. (2008) Research Methodology in the Behaviourial Sciences. Nigeria: Longman Nigeria PLC.

Aydelotte, W.O (1971) Quantification in History. New York: Addison-Wesly Publishing Co.

Aydelotte, W.O. (1966) Quantification in History. The American Historical Review. 71(3):803-825. https://www.jstor.org/stable/1846023

Bailey, K.D. (1982). Methods of Social Research. New York: The Free Press.

Chegwe, E.N (2016) Legal Research Methodology and Project Writing. Ekpoma-Nigeria: Ambrose Alli University Press

Conrad C. (2015) Social History. In James Wright (Ed) Encyclopedia of the Social and Behavioural Sciences. Second Edition. https://doi.org: 10.1016/B978-0-08-097086-8-62127-X pp. 307-312

Desai R. (ND) Relevance of History for Social Research. Accessed at https://www.yourarticlelibrary.com/social-research/relevance-of-history-for-social-research/92785 on 14/03/2021

Ellinger, E.P and Keith, K.J (2015) Legal research: Techniques and ideas. http://14.139.60.114:8080/jspui/bitstream/123456789/18/legal/%20research-techniques%20and%20.ideas.pdf

Gasiokwu, M. U (1994) Legal Research and Methodology. Nigeria: Fab educational books

Gbadesgen, A. and Oyeranti, O. A (2005) Introduction to Social Science and Empirical analysis. In Gbadesgensin, Olopoenia and Jerome (eds) Statistics for the Social Sciences. Ibadan: Ibadan University Press

Gottschalk (1963) Generalisation. In Gottschalk (ed) generalization in the writing of history: A report of the committee on historical analysis of the social sciences. Chicago: the University of Chicago press.

Hays, S. (1994) Historical Social Research: concept method and techniques. Journal of Interdisplinary History. IV (3): 475-482. Doi:10.2307/ 202489. https://www.jstor.org/stable/202489

Hopkins T. (1964) Review of generalization in the writing of history. Political science quarterly. 79:635-638. https://www.jstor.org/stable/2146729

Horwitz, M. J (1977) *The Transformation of American Law, 1780-1860.* Cambridge: Howard University Press.

Karz, M.B (2013) Quantification and the Scientific Study of History. Journal Historical Method. 63-68. https://doi.org/101080100182494.1973.105 93998.

Khushal, V & Philipus, A (2009) Legal Research Methods: Teaching Material. Nigeria: Justice and Legal System Research Institute.

Nowell-Smith, P.H. (1957) Are Historical Events Unique. Proceedings of the Aristotelian Society. New series. Oxford: Oxford University Press

Obasi, I. N (1999) Research Methodology in Political Science. Nigeria: Academic Printing Press.

Odafe, (2003) History. A paper delivered in the Department of History and International Studies. Delta state University Abraka.

Ofo .E. (1994). Research Methods and Statistics. Nigeria: Joja Press.

Oyibo, E .E. (1992). Basic Research and Statistical Methodology for Health and Allied Students. Benin City: A.P.A. Ogefere & Co.

Partington, G.G. (1980) Historical generalization. The history teacher. 13(3):385-400. Doi: 10.2307/491678 https://www.jstor.org/stable/491678

Philips, J. (2010) Why Legal History Matters. *Victoria University of Wellington Law Review.* 41(3) : 293-316. https://doi.org/10.26686/vuwir.v41i3.5 228

Porter, D.M. (1963) Theoretical Generalisation. In Gottschalk (ed) generalization in the writing of history: A report of the committee on historical analysis of the social sciences. Chicago: the University of Chicago press. .

Ruggles, S and Magnuson, D.L (2019) The History of quantification in History: the JIH as a case study. Journal of Interdisciplinary History.50(3):363-381. www.mit.pressjournal.org>doi>fill>jinh=9_01446

Smelser, N. (1959) *Social Change in the Industrial Revolution: An Application of the Theory to the Lancashire Cotton Industry 1770-1840.* London: Routhledge and Kegan Paul.

Smith, K.J.M and McLaren, J.P.S (2001) History's Living Legacy: An Outline of Modern Historiography of the common law. *Legal Studies. Journal of the Society of Legal Scholars.* 21(2): 251-324.

Social Research: Meaning and Definition. www.jayaram.com.ppl/social-researc-meaning-and-definition

Spohn, W (2015) History and the Social Sciences. In James Wright (Ed) Encyclopedia of the Social and Behavioural Sciences. Second Edition.

www.sciencedirect.com/referencework/9780080970875/international-encyclopedia-of-the-social-and -behavioural-sciences

SSRC (2016) History as Social Science. https://item.ssrc.org/from-our-archivrs/history-as-social-science.

Weedon, A. (2019) The uses of Quantification. In Eliot and Jonathan (Eds) A Companion to the history of the book. 2nd edition. https://doi.org/10.1002/9781119018193.ch3

Wilson, H. H. (1887) The relation of History to Study and Practice of Law. Transactions and reports. Nebraska State Historical Society. Vol 2. https://digitalcomanns.un/edu/nebhisttrane/15

# CHAPTER NINE

# FALLACIES IN RESEARCH

Peter Eshioke Egielewa

## Introduction

Research is an important and critical part of human endeavour. It is the process through which humans seeks solutions to questions that plague society. American sociologist Earl Robert Babbie succinctly summarises the main elements of research, namely, "systematic inquiry to describe, explain, predict, and control observed phenomenon" (Toni, Maphosa & Wadesango, 2014; Bhat, 2020). Bhat (2020) explains further that research has four main purposes which are: (1) what does the individual or group want to find out? (2)What are the processes that need to be followed to chase the idea? (3) What are the arguments that need to be built around a concept or arrive at a conclusion? (4) What is the evidence that will be required for people to believe in the idea or concept or in the conclusion? (Bhat, 2020).

The implications of the goals of research show that research is a systematic undertaking with rules and principles guiding its processes up to the point of arriving at findings and conclusions and making recommendations that can be implemented to solve the original problems or gaps for which the research was undertaken in the first place.

When the required research principles and guidelines are not followed, it puts the results of the research into questions and thus renders the entire research efforts in jeopardy making them irrelevant since basic expectations of credible research were not adhered to. This then brings to fore the issue of credibility, namely that the research process lacked credibility and thus renders the research and its findings untenable, un-implementable and to a certain extent even criminal. The problems that can occur in the process of research that can render both the research processes and the findings untenable are called fallacies of research.

## What is a fallacy?

The term "fallacy" can be traced to the late 15th century and comes from the Latin "*fallacia*" meaning "deception, deceit, trick, artifice." Thus, fallacy can be understood to mean "deception, false statement." From the point of view of logic, fallacy means "false syllogism or invalid argumentation." (etymonline.com, 2020). Fallacies are mistakes of reasoning, that is mistaken beliefs based on unsound arguments (Van Cleave, 2020). Fallacies derive from reasoning that is logically incorrect and undermines the validity of an argument.

In general, fallacies are statements that sound reasonable or true but are actually flawed or dishonest and when detected make the writer appear as either deceptive or unintelligent. Fallacies make the arguments of a writer bad and should be avoided (Logical fallacies handlist: arguments to avoid when writing, n.d.).

## Types of fallacies

There are over 200 types of fallacies (Dowden, n.d.) but the major types are selected and discussed below. Fallacies are either formal or informal. Formal fallacies are detected simply by examining the logical form of the reasoning that is an argument whose form can be invalid, irrespective of the meaning of the sentences (Van Cleave, 2020).

Informal fallacies are fallacies which depend on the content of the reasoning and the purpose of the reasoning. In other words, informal fallacies are errors of reasoning that cannot easily be expressed in our system of formal logic. Van Cleave (2020) explains that informal fallacies are those which cannot be identified if the concepts involved in an argument are not properly understood.

Dowden (n.d.), Cook (2018), Purdue University (n.d.) and YourDictionary (n.d.) have grouped into three main categories, namely fallacies of relevance, fallacies of ambiguity and fallacies of presumption.

## A. Fallacies of relevance

These are fallacies that occur due to reliance on an irrelevant reason. Some of these include:

### i. Ad Hominem (attacking the person)

"Ad Hominem" is Latin which means "to the person" or "directed at the person." It is a fallacy that occurs when the reasoning in an argument includes an irrelevant attack on the arguer and suggests that this attack weakens of undermines the validity of the argument itself. For example, one's sex should not be a factor on a lady competence in mathematics. There are five subtypes of Ad Hominem. The first subcategory is Circumstantial Ad Hominem is the type of fallacy that occurs when irrelevant circumstances of an arguer to undermine his reasoning e.g. when it argued that because an arguer has a vested interest in people accepting the position, his reasoning is untenable. The second subcategory of Abusive Ad Hominem occurs when the fallacious attack is directed at some despicable trait of the arguer to undermine the position of the arguer. The third subcategory is Guilt by Association which occurs when an attack is directed at the arguer's associates. The fourth subcategory is called the Genetic Fallacy when the fallacy focuses on a complaint about the origin of the arguer's views and the fifth subcategory is the Tu Quoque which is the fallacy committed when it is claimed that an arguer does not practice what is preached.

### ii. Ad Misericordiam (Appeal to Pity)

This is also called the Fallacy of Appeal to Emotions. This fallacy occurs when someone's appeal to an arguer to accept their claim purely on the basis of an appeal meant to arouse the arguer's feelings of anger, fear, grief, love, outrage, pity, pride, sexuality, sympathy, relief, amongst others. It is fallacious when such emotions are used to downplay relevant information, for example, it during a football match a footballer broke his ankle and demand for a penalty, then the fallacy of Ad misericordiam has been applied.

### iii. Affirming the Consequent

This fallacy occurs when an arguer has enough evidence to affirm the consequent of a conditional argument (if-then and then suppose that as a result, he has sufficient reason to affirm the antecedent. A conditional argument contains the "if-then" statement, where the if-part is the antecedent, and the then-part is the consequent. e.g. If he Nigerian, then he speaks pidgin. Yes, he speaks pidgin, therefore he is Nigerian.

### iv. Appeal to Popular Opinion

This fallacy occurs when arguer relies on the popularity of a view among people to justify why such a position should be accepted. In order word, because many people think that such a position is the best, therefore, it is the best. Support this government's policy since 75% of voters elected the officials.

### v. Appeal to Authority

This fallacy occurs when an arguer attempts to align their arguments with a person in authority to justify the arguer's position. In other words, the argument's credibility rests on what an authority believes or says to convince an opponent to accept a position as correct. e.g. because the president says disinfectants can kill coronavirus, therefore, disinfectants actually kill coronavirus. Do you want to question the president's knowledge?

## B. Fallacies of ambiguity

These are fallacies which involve some level of unclarity language, confusion in words, terms and meanings. These include:

### i. Accent

The Accent Fallacy, which is also called Accentus or Misleading Accent, is a fallacy of ambiguity that arises as a result of the different way a word or syllable is emphasized or accented. For example, in the sentence "Did you mean the invalid one?" emphasis or accent on the first syllable of the word "invalid," refers to "speaking of a sick person" while emphasis or accent on the second syllable of the word "invalid," refers to speaking of an argument failing to meet the deductive standard of being valid.

### ii. Amphiboly

Amphiboly occurs when a grammatically ambiguous phrase is used in two different ways during the reasoning. In other words, it is due to syntactic ambiguity that is caused by multiple ways of understanding the grammar of the phrase. For example, "the boy gives his colleague a hand." (Interpretations: (1) Such a nice fellow helping someone in need (2) How did the boy get a hand to give his colleague? Did he kill someone?). The understanding of the word "hand" was misinterpreted.

### iii. Equivocation

The fallacy of Equivocation occurs due to the illegitimate switching of the meaning of a term that occurs twice during reasoning. In other words, it is the use of one word used in two ways in a reasoning process and can sometimes be very difficult to detect. e.g. "Brad is a nobody, but since nobody is perfect, Brad must be perfect, too." In the above example, the word "nobody" changes its meaning twice in the sentence without warning.

### iv. Straw Man Fallacies

The fallacy of straw man happens when an arguer's opponent over-simplifies or misrepresents an arguer's argument to make it easier to attack or refute it. The fallacy attempts to make the argument of the opponent look weak and to place one's argument in a position of strength and victory over the opponent, e.g. Arguer 1: "Let's go diplomatic with China." Arguer 2: "I can't believe you are this unpatriotic."

## C. Fallacies of presumption

These are fallacies that occur when an unwarranted and unnecessary assumption is the basis for reaching a conclusion.

### i. Begging the Question

This is a form of circular reasoning in which a conclusion is derived from premises that presuppose the conclusion. In the fallacy of begging the question, the arguer starts from a point and ends up at that same point without saying anything new. e.g. "women have rights. But women shouldn't fight bulls because a bullfighter is and should be a man," says the Bullfighters Association president. What the president is saying is that women shouldn't fight bulls because women shouldn't fight bulls. Such reasoning is circular and makes no progress.

### ii. Complex Question

The fallacy of complex question occurs when a question is so framed that some controversial presupposition is made about the wording of the question. e.g. A journalist asks the US president: "Mr. President: Are you going to continue your policy of wasting taxpayer's money on missile defense?." This question is complex because it has already unfairly presumed that the policy is a waste of money. Either way, the president responds he is trapped. The Fallacy of complex question is a form of begging the question.

### iii. Suppressed Evidence

This fallacy occurs when an arguer intentionally fails to use some vital information suspected of being relevant and significant to an argument. Usually, it occurs when the suppressed information or evidence will affect the arguer's position or conclusion. e.g. an arguer argues that buying the Cray Mac 11 computer for his company was the right thing to do because it will meet the company's needs, runs the programs the company wants it to run, costs much less than what had budgeted and fast delivery. This argument sounds good, but the company will probably change its position in buying the Cray MAC 11 if it knew that the arguer has intentionally suppressed the relevant evidence that his company's Cray Mac 11 was purchased from his brother-in-law at a 30 percent higher price than it could have been purchased elsewhere, and that a recent unbiased analysis of ten comparable computers placed the Cray Mac 11 near the bottom of the list.

### iv. Hasty Generalisation

This fallacy occurs when a conclusion is reached based on insufficient, inadequate or biased evidence. In this fallacy, the arguer has some facts of an argument but it is not enough to arrive at the conclusion reached. e.g. All Edo University students wear black and white dresses to classes, whereas the arguer saw only law students (who normally wear white and black dresses to classes) when he visited the university campus and concluded that because all the students he saw on the campus that day wore black and white, therefore all students of the university wear black and white.

## Fallacies of research

Having examined general logical fallacies, it is now relevant to discuss how they relate to research fallacies. For the purpose of this discussion, I would define a research fallacy as an error or defect in a researcher's process of conceiving ideas, developing such ideas, and then writing, creating and publishing that idea as an academic work. Such errors involve the documentation of ideas, appropriate reporting of findings, publishing academic materials that meet expected standards.

### Types of research fallacies

Howard (2016) has researched and identified twelve (12) different types of research fallacies which shall be explained as follows. Howard (2016) classified the research fallacies into three categories: fallacies of authority, fallacies of logic and fallacies of emotion. The different research fallacies will be discussed under the appropriate categories.

### A. Fallacies of Authority

These are fallacies that are usually found in literature reviews.

### i. Straw Man

This fallacy occurs when a researcher intentionally dismisses as unreasonable counterarguments in his work. In this fallacy which is all too common in literature reviews enables the researcher to think that counterarguments are unhelpful to his current research and so discountenance same. In other words, the researchers downplay academic works that are critical of his positions or views. This is a fallacy because every research is a synthesis of a thesis and an antithesis, where research can often negate the hypothesis of current research. This is the reason why a deliberate ignoring of critical counterarguments is a major fallacy of research.

### ii. Irrelevant Conclusion

This research fallacy is often not intentional and it occurs when there is an accidental omission of vital information that helps readers connect between the points made and the conclusion. In other words, the missing points make it difficult for the reader to be able to understand how the author jumped from the findings to the conclusion. In such cases, the conclusions may have little or nothing to do with the line of arguments up to the conclusion. As mentioned earlier, this may be due to inexperience in linking findings to the conclusion or weak conclusions. In general, this fallacy is not intentional on the part of the author. For instance, "because students who are tall, they must be intelligent." In this instance, the author does not justify how being tall as a student means the student will be intelligent.

### iii. Killing the Messenger

This research fallacy occurs when the author leaves the main *kern* of an argument in a study and attacks the author of the argument. In this context, when an author uses such adjectives as "feminists," "sadists" "conservatives," or "pessimists," they are actively committing the fallacy of killing the messenger. In other words, the author focuses so much on an author's personality rather than on the issues being argued in the study. In general, the personality of an opponent is attacked when the opponent has a different position, ideology or view of a theme to which the author has little or no strong counter-arguments (or he may have) but believes an attack on the personality of the arguer will be the most potent weapon to discredit the author' position. This fallacy is common in the divergent approaches to research questions. Examples are: "Lucy will definitely hold that position because she is a feminist" or "John's position is expected because he holds conservative views."

### iv. Faulty Authority

This research fallacy occurs when a wrong authority is cited to justify an author's position. Many authors commit this fallacy especially when the cited author is well known in his field and therefore they have the false illusion that citing such an author gives credence to their line of argument. However, such constitutes a fallacy because an author can only be cited as an authority in his fields of specialisation and no other irrespective of how popular such an author may be. This fallacy occurs in two forms in academic research: (a) if a researcher uses such phrase as "studies show" whereas the author does not, in fact, cite any particular author and (b) when an author cites very well-known authors like Abraham Maslow or Marshall McLuhan to justify their argument whereas in actual fact the ideas of such authors were never used.

## B. Fallacies of Logic

These are fallacies that are usually found in explanations of research questions, hypotheses and findings.

### i. Correlation is not Causation

This research fallacy occurs when an author assumes that because two events happen in quick succession, the first is the cause of the other. For example, since a bottle of poisonous liquid was found in the room of the deceased, therefore the deceased died of self-poison whereas in actual fact the bottle of poison being close to the corpse of the deceased may, upon investigation, be discovered not to have anything to do with the person's death.

Conversely, the real causal link is possible and should not be discountenanced or ignored too. For instance, if students are allowed to drink alcohol on campus and violent incidences on campus increases, there may indeed be actual connections and should not be ignored but investigated. The fallacy is common in social sciences that use correlational statistical methods.

### ii. Begging the Question

This fallacy usually occurs when a researcher assumes that an audience will not be able to decipher when he tries to play on their intelligence by not attempting to address the research questions set out to be investigated but simply advances justifications many of which do not answer the research questions but seek to confuse the audience. For examples when a researcher writes "it is obvious that the man died of poison because poison kills" whereas he has not proven that it was the poison that killed the man misreads their audience, treating an arguable proposition as if it were a fact.

### iii. Hasty Generalization

Generalisations are in themselves not fallacies as along as such generalisation are based on empirical findings. However, if a researcher generalises to prove a point for its own sake, and when the results are not representative enough then the fallacy of hasty generalisation is committed. Authors use hasty generalisations in their conclusion when they try to convince their readers that their research findings are important.

For example, if after an election of a Nigerian state governor in which there are 1, 000, 000 voters is conducted and the author concludes that based on 400, 000 results turned in, candidate A who scores 201, 000 is the winner of the legion, such a generalisation would be fallacious.

### iv. Circular Logic

Circular logic is fallacious because they occur in arguments in which the authors do not offer points to support their arguments but simply restate their departure points. For example, "to overcome failures in examinations, students should read for at least three hours daily because reading three hours a day gives a student outstanding success" or "to be successful in marriage, love and faithfulness are two very key requirements because as long as there is love and faithfulness between a married couple such a marriage will be hugely successful."

## C. Fallacies of Emotion

These are fallacies of emotion which are usually found in grant proposals or public scholarships, such as reports to funders, policymakers, employers, journalists, and the public.

### i. Appeal to Tradition

This fallacy occurs when researchers try to justify their methodology for research by arguing that a particular method is common and is used in several previous kinds of research whereas it may not be appropriate in the present context but the authors rely on the long use of that methodology as a justification for their choice of the same methodology.

Conversely, some authors can argue for the new. They could argue that since the methodology is new, current and trendy then they want to use it. They may argue that many recent kinds of research rely on that methodology and present that as a justification for their choice of the methodology for their research.

### ii. Appeal to Pride

This fallacy occurs when scholars assume that their methods of research are the most reliable in their fields of studies. They may claim that to study certain phenomena, their methods are the most or sometimes only appropriate methods to be used otherwise results arrived at would not be reliable. For instance, some authors have argued that to study certain phenomena only the quantitative approach is suitable or only the qualitative approach or only the critical discourse analysis (CDA) is the most appropriate. This smirks off academic pride because research is flexible and there is creativeness in the selection of methods for research.

### iii. Appeal to Pity

This fallacy occurs when authors try to whip up sentiments towards the subject of their research. It can indeed happen that the subject of research involves marginalised or minority groups but when authors deliberately use such sentiments to evoke acceptance of their conclusions and ignoring the normal processes of evaluating research works, then such authors commit this fallacy. For instance, when a researcher concludes thus: "the poor needs help and these research findings will help them." this fallacy is committed.

### iv. Appeal to Popular Opinion

This fallacy is among the most common fallacies committed by researchers and also one of the hardest to prevent. This fallacy attempts to follow the academic culture of "this is how it has always been done." In the sense, it is argued that the way everyone does it must be correct and the right way. For example when an author cites every word found in consulted works. It can be equated with the popular advertiser's fallacy that "A million users can't be wrong" This fallacy usually occurs in literature review and can be found in two forms, namely: (a) the academic culture of citing several authors without elaborating on specific findings and (b) the practice of offering a citation to other authors' literature review, review essay or meta-analysis.

### D. Individual-based fallacies

The two fallacies in this category are proposed by Trochim (2020) and labelled individual-based fallacies for the purpose of this study because they are based on how researchers relate cases in research to individuals in groups and can be fallacious. This thus brings the total number of research fallacies to fourteen (14) discussed in the study.

### i. Ecological fallacy

The ecological fallacy occurs when researchers make conclusions about individuals based only on analyses of information from a group. It is a form of hasty generalisation but in this case, it occurs when information of the group is transferred to the individual in the group. For example, because Edo University students are hardworking students does not mean that all Edo university students are hard working. It will, therefore, be an ecological fallacy to assume that because it has been established that Edo University Iyamho students are hardworking means that the next student of Edo University Iyamho that comes around for a meeting is hard working.

### ii. Exception fallacy

The exception fallacy is the opposite of the ecological fallacy. This fallacy occurs when based on findings of exceptional cases, a conclusion is reached about the entire group. This fallacy is the basis for racism and much gender-based discrimination. For example, if a researcher concludes that because the percentage of blacks involved in crimes in the American city of Chicago has doubled over the last ten years, therefore blacks in America are criminals whereas Chicago is just one of the thousands of American cities and statistics from Chicago may not be the true reflection of the behaviour of blacks in other cities of America.

## Theoretical Framework: Elaboration Likelihood Model (ELM)

The Elaboration Likelihood Model was developed by Richard Petty and John Cacioppo in 1986 (Petty & Cacioppo, 1986; Bitner & Obermiller, 1985; OER Services, 2020). It is a dual-process theory of attitude formation and change built on the understanding that individuals can be influenced to change their attitude towards a certain object, events, or behaviour and the relative efficacy of such change strategies. The authors argue that the attitude of an individual may be shaped by two types of influences depending on the amount of information processing and elaboration required of the parties involved, namely; the central route and the peripheral route.

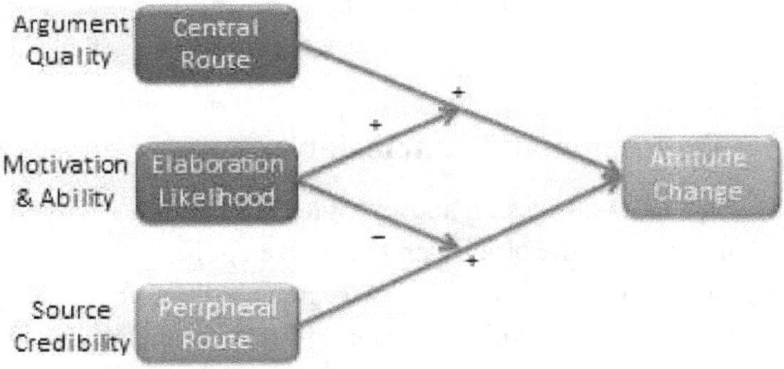


**Figure 1. Elaboration likelihood model.**
**Source: www. lumenlearning.com**

The central route requires an individual to reflect on issue-related arguments in an informational message and carefully scrutinize the merits and relevance of such arguments, before arriving at an informed judgment about the target object. In other words, people's attitudes are formed and changed as a result of careful consideration and integration of information that is relevant to the object or issue being argued for or against (Bitner & Obermiller, 1985). On the peripheral route, individuals depend on external forces to make them change their attitudes toward an issue such as the number of prior users, endorsements from experts, or likeability of the endorser, rather than on the quality of arguments.

An individual's adoption of either of the routes depends principally on their ability and motivation to elaborate on the central merits of an argument. Such ability and motivation to elaborate is called elaboration likelihood. Individual who possess a higher level of elaboration likelihood is more likely to thoughtfully process the information presented and be influenced by the quality of an argument while individuals with lower elaboration likelihood are more motivated by peripheral factors (Lien, 2001, OER Services, 2020). Elaboration likelihood is situational and context-dependent and not a personal trait. For examples, a doctor needs the central route to diagnose and treat his patients but he needs the peripheral cues from auto mechanics to understand and fix his car problems (Lien, 2001, OER Services, 2020).

The theory of the Elaboration Likelihood Model (ELM) is apt for this study of fallacies in research because the knowledge of research fallacies will enable authors to make attitudinal changes in the way they approach research.

## Discussion and conclusion

From the discussion above, logic constitutes an essential aspect of arguments and it is the orderly and effective application of arguments that helps researchers to present their research work to their audiences in a clear, transparent and ethical manner. While it appears that the average researcher knows and understands the nuances of what research entails, some authors may be engaging in research which they are not. Some scholars (O'Donnell, 2012; Leite, 2014; Bhat, 2020) have explained what research is not. Since research is a systematic enquiry that entails processing data and analysing them to contribute to society's development (Hampshire College, 2020), undertaking such a noble exercise while at the same time violating the core research principles leads to the risk of committing a fallacy which weakens the credibility of a research endeavour and renders such a research work not only weak but the findings questionable and untenable. Fallacies are logical errors in arguments and since arguments are the basis of academic work, logical errors can indeed constitute a huge barrier to the presentation of thought processes in an orderly, logical and comprehensive way. To avoid such pitfalls in research,

Bhat (2020) has identified key characteristics. This notwithstanding, more harmful in research, however, are research fallacies, fourteen of which have been enumerated by some scholars (Howard, 2016; Trochim, 2020) and discussed in this study. Research fallacies are not exhaustive in themselves but can act as a springboard to evaluating other research fallacies. Research fallacies, however, in general, create credibility problems for research work and their knowledge and avoidance are therefore important steps in writing a fallacy-free and society impactful research work. The aspect of research which allows an author concentrate on issues related argument in arriving at decision including research judgement is the central point of the central route of the Elaboration Likelihood Model as espoused by Richard Petty and John Cacioppo in 1986 (Petty & Cacioppo, 1986; Bitner & Obermiller, 1985; OER Services, 2020). Consequently, the Elaboration Likelihood Model was used to justify this study.

## Recommendations

Based on the study, the following can be recommended.

1. Academic and other researchers should study the types of logical fallacies and avoid them in their researches.
2. Researchers should know and understand how to avoid research fallacies.
3. Peer reviewers of academic works should know the several research fallacies and point them out in works reviewed for the attention of the authors.

## References

Bhat, A. (2020). What is research? Definition, methods, types & examples. https://www.questionpro.com/blog/what-is-research/

Bitner, M. J. & Obermiller, C. (1985). The Elaboration Likelihood Model: Limitations and extensions in marketing. *Association for Consumer Research, 12*, 420-425.

Cook, K. (2018). 15 common logical fallacies and how to spot them. https://blog.hubspot.com/marketing/common-logical-fallacies

Dowden, B. (n.d.). Fallacies. *Internet Encyclopedia of Philosophy*. https://www.iep.utm.edu/fallacy/Etymonline.com. (2020). Fallacy. https://www.etymonline.com/word/fallacy

Hampshire College. (2020). What is research? https://www.hampshire.edu/dof/what-is-research

Howard, P. (2016). 12 common fallacies used in social research. https://medium.com/@pnhoward/12-common-fallacies-used-in-social-research-9713e4d9bf48

Inductive or Deductive? Two Different Approaches. (n.d). Retrieved on 1 July 2020 from https://saylordotorg.github.io/text_principles-of-sociological-inquiry - qualitative-and - quantitative-methods / s05-03-inductive-or-deductive-two-dif.html

Leite, S. (2014). What research is not and what it is. https://educatinginternationally.wordpress.com/2014/04/22/what-research-is-not-and-what-it-is/

Lien, N. (2001). Elaboration Likelihood Model in consumer research: A review. *Proceedings of the National Science Council, 11* (4), 301-310.

Logical fallacies handlist: Arguments to avoid when writing. (n.d.). Retrieved on 1 July 2020 from https://web.cn.edu/kwheeler/documents/Logic_Fallacies_List.pdf

O'Donnell, J. (2012). What is research? https://researchwhisperer.org/2012/09/18/what-is-research/

OER Services. (2020). Theories in scientific research. https://courses.lumenlearning.com/suny-hccc-research-methods / chapter/chapter-4-theories-in-scientific-research/

Petty, R.E. & Cacioppo, J.T. (1986). The Elaboration Likelihood Model of Persuasion. In *Communication and Persuasion: Springer Series in Social Psychology* (pp. 1-24). Springer. Purdue University. (n.d.). Logical fallacies.

https://owl.purdue.edu/owl/general_writing/academic_writing/logic_in_argumentative_writing/fallacies.html

The Nature and tools of research. (n.d.) Retrieved on 1 July 2020 from http://bentonenglish.com/wp-content/uploads/2017/08/What-Research-Is-Not-Is.pdf

Toni, N., Maphosa, C. & Wadesango, N. (2014). Promoting the interplay between teaching and research in the university and the role of the academic developer. *Mediterranean Journal of Social Sciences, 5*(11), 19-27.

Trochim, W. M. K. (2020). Two research fallacies. https://conjointly.com/kb/two-research-fallacies/#:~:text=Two%20Research%20Fallacies-,Two%20Research%20Fallacies,usually%20based%20on%20mistaken%20assumptions.&text=The%20ecological%20fallacy%20occurs%20when,on%20analyses%20of%20group%20data.

Van Cleave, M. (2020). Formal versus informal fallacies. https://human.libretexts.org/Bookshelves/Philosophy/Book%3A_Introduction_to_Logic_and_Critical_Thinking_(van_Cleave)/04%3A_Informal_Fallacies/4.01%3A_Formal_vs._Informal_Fallacies

Your Dictionary. (n.d.). Types of logical fallacies. https://examples.yourdictionary.com/examples-of-logical-fallacy.html

# CHAPTER TEN
# REFERENCING STYLES

**Florence Masajuwa**

## Introduction

The idea of referencing is as old as academic writing. Academic writing itself evolved from research. When one carries out research, one inevitably queries what others have said or written about that particular issue or aspects of it one is investigating. In order words, research entails investigating what other scholars have said about the topic one is interested in (William, 2014). Both referencing and academic writing was born out of the desire to document as well as connect one research finding to one or other research findings. As research writers cut across various academic fields, so also, there is no agreement among them regarding the form of referencing system, they should adopt to connect earlier sources in their writings. Thus, each field in reporting their research findings, devised ways unique to that field, of linking current results to previous ones. This scenario led to the multiplicity of referencing styles or systems.

This chapter examines referencing styles or systems used in academic writings. However, only referencing styles applicable to the social sciences, humanities, management, and legal studies will be examined. In this time of information and communication technology (ICT) and the attendant internet revolution, it's pertinent that any writing on citations and referencing systems must also encompass an examination of online referencing management tools like Endnote, Zotero, Mendeley, etc. To this end, the chapter examines the definition, meaning, and historical evolution of referencing. Next, we discussed why referencing is necessary, the different types of referencing systems, citing examples for easy understanding. Finally, the chapter examined some online referencing tools like EndNote, Zotero, and Mendeley.

## Evolution of Referencing in Academic Writing

There are different forms of writings, for example, academic writing, creative writing, business writing, and legal writing among others. Each form of writing one way or the other, may draw inspiration from an earlier writing or Work. Referencing is what links one writing to the other. It also distinguishes academic writing from the other forms of writing. Most academic writings are aftermaths of researches carried out by individuals or groups. The term research in the academic circles means re-examining a phenomenon or an aspect of that phenomenon. The essence is to enhance the understanding of the phenomenon or to debunk outrightly the tenets on which the phenomenon is built.

The ideas inherent in the phenomenon under examination is documented. In order to build on the new effort directed at enhancing or discrediting tenets of the erstwhile phenomenon, recurs must be made to those documents that gave spur to the original phenomenon. This is the ideal informing the idea of referencing. In effect, the new effort must acknowledge that it is built from the original phenomenon its re-examining. In acknowledging the initial efforts, the new effort must do so in recognised and accepted formats specified for doing so.

## Definition of terms

### Citation

Citation is presented inside the text as one writes, to indicate information taken from other sources such as quotes or an idea.

### Reference, Reference List and Bibliography

**Reference** is meant to give full details of the source of information in a research paper. Depending on the referencing system used, reference could be fixed at the end of a write up or chapter, or sometimes at the bottom of each page. On the other hand, a **reference list** is a list at the end of a chapter or essay giving full details of sources cited within the essay. **A bibliography** is a list at the end of a research paper which gives the full details of all sources which the writer may have read even if they are not referred to within the text (University of Leeds Library, 2020).

In this chapter, referencing means acknowledging the Work of others used in one's own Work. The works acknowledged may be in the form of ideas, texts, pictures, paintings, drawings, performance, sound, information etc. In effect, in all academic writings, it is apposite that one references any work paraphrased, quoted or summarised (2012).

Two elements that are crucial to referencing include:

- An in-text citation
- An entry in the reference list at the end of one's paper or written term paper assignment. Quite often the citation do provide adequate details that will enable a reader to easily identify the sources listed in the list of references (Bachelorprint, n.d)

To University Kent, (2012) "referencing means acknowledging your source: in the body of your work (in-text referencing or citation) and linking your citations to your list of works cited (also reference list or bibliography)."

The University of West Minister (2006), explained the concept of referencing as acknowledging the ideas of others such as quotations, the information we used in our Work. On his part, Lipson (2011:3) used the term "citation" in place of referencing and opined that it means giving credit to others whether we agree or not with their works, by citing their works properly, putting their exact words in quotation marks, etc.

To Neville (2010: 3), referencing has four components, namely 3Ws & H. These components stand for:

The "*why*" of referencing: the academic rationale for all styles of referencing and the principles underpinning the practice.

The "what" of referencing: what to reference, which sources to choose.

The "*when*" of referencing: when to reference – and when it is not necessary.

And the "*how*" of referencing which describes the main differences between referencing styles.

This chapter's focus is on the "when" and "how" of reference. While the "when" of referencing explains why we reference, the "how" describes the various styles of referencing in the academic circles. Thus, we can say referencing is one of the fundamental requirements in academic writing (Moor, Neville & Murphy, 2010:98).

## Style or System

Various sources have defined the word style. To Longman Dictionary (2020), style means a particular way of doing, designing, or producing something, especially one that is typical of a particular place, period of time, or group of people. The style also means the way in which something is said, done, expressed, or performed (Free Dictionary, 2020).

The Oxford English and Spanish Dictionary say the word style is a particular procedure by which something is done; a manner or way. To the creators of the APA referencing style, the American Psychological Association (APA), style refers to guidelines for ensuring clear, consistent communication and presentation in written works. From all these definitions, style means the method of doing things that is unique to a set of people or organisations.

**A System** is defined as a set of principles or procedures according to which something is done; an organized scheme or method (Oxford Dictionary, 2020). The system means to program, organisation, arrangement, classification, structure, and process.

In this chapter, style is used interchangeably with the system. In effect, form or system is used in the same sense as a method, methodology, technique, process, arrangement, and procedure.

## Referencing Style

In their essay entitled 'referencing and citation,' Bachelorprint (Bachelorprint, 2020) defined referencing styles as "a set of rules that tell you how you should acknowledge the intellectual works of people that you use in your research reports."

On their part, the University of Queensland Library (2020), defined a referencing style as "a set of rules on how to acknowledge the thoughts, ideas, and works of others in a particular way."

## Why We Reference

There are many reasons why one must reference when writing academic papers. Your paper is more respected in the academic circle. Also, the writer becomes recognised and respected among your intellectual community. You are seen as a person of high intellectual integrity, thus avoiding the disdain that accompanies plagiarism. Future researchers feel more comfortable using research papers with references. Through referencing, future researchers can easily cross-check the facts and theories in the earlier Work through the works cited. Also, prospective researchers desirous of replicating a particular research work in another jurisdiction or location will trust a paper that has discernable references.

Explaining the importance of referencing even in students class assignments such as term papers, Moore et al (2010:109) had this to say:

Accurate referencing enhances your authority as a writer and steers you away from plagiarism. Referencing your sources accurately indicates to your tutors that you have researched the assignment topic; it properly acknowledges the hard Work of the original authors; and it helps other people to locate the same sources for their own learning purposes. It also strengthens your own voice in assignments, as you can use sources to support your own ideas or arguments.

## Referencing Systems

There are several referencing systems. Also, creators of each referencing system often come up with new editions of their reference style. However, the existence of many referencing styles and various versions have become a source of concern to many writers who often get confused as to which of the forms and editions they should follow in their research writings (Richard & Graham, 2010: 3).

The good thing, however, is that the editorial boards of most journals often indicate the type of referencing style and the Edition to use in articles to be published in their journals. This information is usually contained in the inside cover page of most journals under the heading' Guide to Article contributors.' The preferred referencing style and the Edition are among the items listed in the guide to contributors.

Also, the existence of many styles of referencing is because most professional bodies come up with a referencing style they consider as meeting the peculiar needs of their profession. Some examples will suffice here to illustrate the point being made. At the international level, we have APA referencing style developed and used by the American Psychological Association (APA), the Bluebook developed by the American Bar, the MLA developed by the Modern Language Association, etc. Back home in Nigeria, we have the NALT Greenbook referencing Manual developed by the Nigerian Association of Law Teachers (NALT) and being used by law teachers and students in writing academic papers in legal studies.

Notwithstanding the variations in referencing styles, the three most used across disciplines include APA, Chicago, and MLA (Lipson, 2006:5). All the others are variants of one or the other of these three. Each of these variants requires that academic writers show the sources used inside their text (citation) and after the writing, compile in alphabetical order, a comprehensive list of all those sources cited-in-text.

Generally, the various referencing styles have been grouped into two major classes. While Moore et al. (2010:114) classified them as "the name and number referencing styles," Williams (2014) preferred to name his categories as "author-date and footnote-bibliography" referencing styles as set out in the Chicago Manual of Style.

### a. Name or Author-Date Referencing Styles

The referencing styles that use the name referencing include the American

1) American Psychological Association (APA) style
2) Modern Language Association (MLA) style
3) The Harvard style

Under these three referencing styles, citing sources in the main body of the write-up entails first, writing the first name or sure-name of the author, followed by the year the Work being cited was published and the page number if the cited Work is printed (Moor et al, 2010:113). After the write-up, all the sources cited in-text, that is, inside the body of the write-up, are compiled in alphabetical order as either a referencing list or a bibliography.

### b. The Number or Footnote-Bibliography Referencing Style

Under Number (Numeric) referencing style, Arabic numbers are used consecutively either concurrently or recurrently in the body of the article being written to identify sources of document consulted, or the issues sought to be clarified and emphasised. In effect, "the citation is a number that refers the reader to a corresponding reference in your reference list. The first source cited in your Work is allocated number 1; the second is allocated number 2, and so on" (University of Leeds, 20-20)

The Concurrent Number Referencing is used in the following:

1) Chicago (or Turabian) style.
2) OSCOLA (Oxford Standard for Citation of Legal Authorities) style.
3) NALT ( Nigerian Association of Law Teachers) style

On the other hand, the recurrent number referencing according to Moore et. al., (2010:114) is used by:

- British Standard (Numeric) style.
- Vancouver style. (Also known as Citation-Sequence system)
- IEEE (Institute of Electrical and Electronics Engineers) style.
- CSE (Council of Science Editors) style

This chapter's area of interest is with the number referencing that uses the concurrent numbering, that is, the Chicago, OSCOLA, and NALT. This of course is in addition to the styles that use the name-date format. These days, each of the styles is used outside their original fields. For example, APA is widely used by most disciplines in the social sciences, Education, Engineering, and Business, MLA in the humanities. Many fields, such as law, use the Chicago style (Lipson, 2006:5).

## Examples of Citations and Referencing Styles

This section examines how in-text-citation and referencing of books, articles, unpublished works, internet sources, and advertisements are done by APA, Chicago, MLA, OSCOLA (including Bluebook developed by Law faculty of Harvard University) and NALT referencing systems. In these days of information and communication technology (ICT) revolution, the various bodies responsible for the plethora of referencing systems often carry out periodic reviews of the styles so as not to only bring them up to date, but also to make them relevant to the contemporary realities of ICT driven world. Thus, the successive editions of Manual of Style of the various citation and referencing systems are prepared with an eye toward how we find, create, and cite information that readers are likely to access from their pockets as from a bookshelf.

The American Psychological Association released its latest APA manual, the 7th Edition on the first of October 2019. However, the 6th Edition, published in 2009, is still used by many universities and journals. It is the style manual of choice for writers, researchers, editors, students, and educators in the social and behavioral sciences, natural sciences, nursing, communications, education, business, engineering, and other fields. Examples of APA referencing styles in this chapter are taken from the current 7th Edition of APA.

For the others, we also drew our samples from their latest editions. The newest Edition of MLA is the 8th Edition, which replaced the Seventh Edition in April 2016. This updated version reflects the ways in which digital publication has changed how writers and researchers document sources (Lipson, 2006: 8).

Examples of Chicago citations are from the authoritative Chicago Manual of Style. The authorities of the University of Chicago released the 17th Edition in 2017 to replace the preceding 16th Edition. The latest editions of OSCOLA and NALT are the 4th and 2nd editions, respectively. The Bluebook is the style manual for citing legal documents within the United States. It is now in its 20th Edition.

## APA System of Citation and Referencing

As explained earlier, all examples of the APA style are as written in the most recent Edition, the 7th Edition. Examined in this segment are examples of APA's citations and referencing styles for books, articles, unpublished works, and websites. (For detailed information on quotes and referencing style of APA, see chapter 10 of American Psychological Manual, 2020, volume 7).

### 1. In-Text Citation

### One Author

a. (Masajuwa, 2020). This is the case in the *parenthetical* style, whereby the author's name and publication year are contained within brackets.
b. Masajuwa (2020) asserted that…,. This is an example of the *narrative* style where the author's name forms part of the sentence while the publication year is in brackets.

### Two Authors

a. (Masajuwa & Imoisi, 2019)- Use the ampersand (&) to connect the two authors in the parenthetical style
b. Masajuwa and Imoisi (2019) argued against NDDC. Use "and" to join the authors in the narrative style

### Three or more Authors

In either case, parenthetical and narrative, only the first authors name is used followed by et al.

a. Parenthetical -(Moore et al., 2010)
b. Narrative- Moore et al. (2010) opine that…

### Group Authors

a. First time it is being cited with an abbreviation:
(Nigerian Association of Law Teachers [NALT], 2019)
b. Then, in subsequent citations that follows.
(NALT, 2019)

### From Citation-in-Text to Reference List under APA Reference Style

The examples of the citations-in- text is given above are now compiled in alphabetical order as references for all the works cited in the write-up.

### 1. Journals

One Author

Masajuwa, F.U. (2020). Beyond Ogoni clean –up: Rethinking environmental protection laws governing the operations of the oil industry in Nigeria. *Petroleum Technology Development Journal.10* (1), 27-44

Two Authors

Masajuwa, F.U. & Imoisi, S. (2019). Rights of host communities to the benefits of Nigeria's oil industry: An appraisal based on international legal standards. *Petroleum Technology Development Journal. 9* (2), 60-73

## 2. Books

a. Without DOI (Digital Object Identifiers)

Umukoro, N. (2018). *State, economy and security in Nigeria.* Benin City: Allen Publications.

Lipson, C. (2011). Cite right: A quick guide to citation styles--MLA, APA, Chicago, the sciences, professions, and more. University of Chicago Press

b. With DOI (Digital Object Identifiers)

Davis, J. R. (2018). *Classroom management in teacher education programs*. Palgrave MacMillan. https://doi.org/10.1007/978-3-319-63850-8 (Strachlide University, Glasgow, 2020)

## 1. Chapter in Edited Book

-Without DOI

Masajuwa, F.U. (2010). Gender equality and the challenges of mobilizing women for national development. In J. Osuntokun, V. Ukogo & A. Odoemene, (Eds.), *Nigerian studies: Readings in history, politics, society, and culture* (pp.219-239). Goldline & Jacobs.

Musa, R. J., & Umukoro, N. (2014). Socio-economic inequality and progress toward achieving education for all by 2015 in Nigeria. In T. Falola & J. Abidogun, (Eds.). *Education, Creativity, and Economic Empowerment in Africa* (pp. 31-41). Palgrave Macmillan.

-With DOI

Pidd, M. (2016). Wearable Books. In R. E. Lyons and S. J. Rayner (Eds). *The academic book of the future* (pp. 18-23). Palgrave Macmillan. https://doi.org/10.1057/9781137595775.0007

## 2. Newspapers and Unpublished Works

**Newspapers**- (Include the web address if Edition used is online)

J. Ajom. (2020, July 30). Westerhof sues Bonfrere over allegations of match-fixing. *Vanguard.* https://www.vanguardngr.com/ 2020/07/westerhof-sues-bonfrere-over- allegations-of-match-fixing/

**Unpublished Work** – (Dissertations, Theses, projects, term papers etc.)

## Table 1- Format for Unpublished Work

| Author | Date | Title | Source |
|---|---|---|---|
| A.A | 2020 | Title of Thesis (Unpublished Master) | Name of School awarding the degree |

**Source: American Psychological Association. (2020) APA Manual (7th Edition). Ch. 10, topic 64**

Masajuwa, F.U. (2015). Legal analyses of the relationship between the multinational oil industry and host communities: A study of Nigeria's Niger Delta (Unpublished doctoral dissertation). The University of Abuja.

### 5. Web Page

Nigerian Bar Association [NBA](2020). List of eligible voters for the 2020 NBA general elections. https://nigerianbar.org.ng/

### Chicago System of Citation and Referencing

The Chicago system of referencing was developed in 1906 by the University of Chicago. Now in its seventeenth Edition, The citation chapters reflect the ever-expanding universe of electronic sources—including social media posts and comments, private messages, and app content—and also offer updated guidelines on such issues as DOIs, time stamps, and e-book locators (University of Oregon Library, 2020).

The Chicago style avails users' two basic ways of referencing their Work, *the author-date* and the *notes and bibliography* referencing. The note and bibliography style has two forms: i). Full first notes ii). Short notes. Each of the two ways often ends with bibliographic entries (Lipson, 2006:13). While many in the humanities, for example, literature, history, and the arts use mostly the *notes and bibliography* style, the author-date-style has long been used by those in the physical, natural, and social sciences.

### 1. Example of Chicago's Author-Date Style

The *author-date* system has similar features as the APA style. Sources are briefly cited in the text, usually in parentheses, by author's last name and date of publication. The short citations are next written out in full and made into a list of references at the end.

### Table 2- Chicago's Author-Date Style

| Author/ Date Style | In-text Citation | Bibliography |
|---|---|---|
| A book | (Pollan 2006, 99–100) | Pollan, Michael. 2006. *The Omnivore's Dilemma: A Natural History of Four Meals*. New York: Penguin. |
| An article in a print journal | (Weinstein 2009, 440) | Weinstein, Joshua I. 2009. "The Market in Plato's *Republic*." *Classical Philology* 104:439–58. |
| An article in an electronic journal | (Kossinets and Watts 2009, 411) | Kossinets, Gueorgi, and Duncan J. Watts. 2009. "Origins of Homophily in an Evolving Social Network." *American Journal of Sociology* 115:405–50. Accessed February 28, 2010. doi:10.1086/599247. |
| A website | (Google 2009) | Google. 2009. "Google Privacy Policy." Last modified March 11. http://www.google.com/intl/en/privacypolicy.html. |

**(Source: Official Chicago Manual website cited in the University of Pittsburg. (2020). Citation Styles: APA, MLA, Chicago, Turabian, IEEE: MLA 8th Edition. Retrieved Friday, July 31, 2020, from https://pitt.libguides.com/citationhelp/mla8thedition.**

### 2. Example of Chicago's Note-Bibliography Style

Under this style of referencing, sources referred to are presented in notes which in most cases are compiled as a bibliography list.

### Table 3- Chicago's Note-Bibliography Style

| Material Type | Notes/Bibliography Style |
|---|---|
| **A book in print** | Note Style: 1. Michael Pollan, *The Omnivore's Dilemma: A Natural History of Four Meals* (New York: Penguin, 2006), 99–100. |

| | |
|---|---|
| | Duplicate Note: 2. Pollan, *Omnivore's Dilemma,* 3. Bibliography: Pollan, Michael. *The Omnivore's Dilemma: A Natural History of Four Meals*. New York: Penguin, 2006. |
| **An article in a print journal** | Note Style: 1. Joshua I. Weinstein, "The Market in Plato's *Republic*," *Classical Philology* 104 (2009): 440. Duplicate Note: 2. Weinstein, "Plato's *Republic*," 452–53. Bibliography: Weinstein, Joshua I. "The Market in Plato's *Republic*." *Classical Philology* 104 (2009): 439–58. |
| **An article in an electronic journal** | Note Style: 1. Gueorgi Kossinets and Duncan J. Watts, "Origins of Homophily in an Evolving Social Network," *American Journal of Sociology* 115 (2009): 411, accessed February 28, 2010, doi:10.1086/599247. Duplicate Note: Kossinets and Watts, "Origins of Homophily," 439. Bibliography: Kossinets, Gueorgi, and Duncan J. Watts. "Origins of Homophily in an Evolving Social Network." *American Journal of Sociology* 115 (2009): 405–50. Accessed February 28, 2010. doi: 10.1086/599247. |
| **A website** | Note Style: 1. "Google Privacy Policy," last modified March 11, 2009, http://www.google.com/intl/en/privacypolicy.html. Duplicate Note: "Google Privacy Policy." Bibliography: Google. "Google Privacy Policy." Last modified March 11, 2009. http://www.google.com/intl/en/privacypolicy.html. |

**(Source: Official Chicago Manual website cited in the University of Pittsburg. (2020). Citation Styles: APA, MLA, Chicago, Turabian, IEEE: MLA 8th Edition. https://pitt.libguides.com/citationhelp/mla8thedition (Accessed, Friday, July 31, 2020)**

## MLA System of Citation and Referencing

Below are some examples of MLA style citations. All examples are as presented in the 8th Edition of MLA Style Manual (University of Pittsburg Library, 2020).

## Table 4- MLA In-text Citation

| Material Type | In-text Citation |
|---|---|
| **Author's name in text** | Magny develops this argument (67-69). |

| | |
|---|---|
| **Author's name in reference** | This argument has been developed elsewhere (Magny 67-69). |
| **Two authors' names in reference** | The most notorious foreign lobby in Washington is the "Sugar Mafia" (Howe and Trott 134). |
| **Quotation found in indirect or "secondhand" source** | The philosopher Alain states that "admiration is not pleasure but a kind of attention. . ." (qtd. in Magny 66). |

## MLA Works Cited Page

MLA style, requires the development of a "Works Cited" page at the end of the paper. A Works Cited page is an alphabetical listing of the resources cited in an academic paper.

## Table 5- MLA Works Cited Page

| Material Type | Works Cited |
|---|---|
| **Book in print** | Card, Claudia. *The Atrocity Paradigm: A Theory of Evil*. Oxford UP, 2005. |
| **eBook** | Gaither, Milton. *Homeschool: An American History*. Palgrave Macmillan, 2017. *SpringerLink*, doi-org.pitt.idm.oclc.org/10.1057/978-1-349-95056-0. |
| **An article in a print journal** | Doggart, Julia. "Minding the Gap: Realizing Our Ideal Community Writing Assistance Program." *The Community Literacy Journal,* vol. 2, no. 1, 2007, pp. 71-80. |
| **An article in an electronic journal** | Sherrard-Johnson, Cherene. "'A Plea for Color': Nella Larsen's Iconography of the Mulatta." *American Literature*, vol. 76, no. 4, 2004, pp. 833-869, doi: 10.1215/00029831-76-4-833. |
| **A encyclopedia entry** | "Patanjali." *Benét's Reader's Encyclopedia,* edited by Bruce Murphy, 4th ed., HarperCollins Publishers, 1996, p. 782. |
| **A government publication** | United States, Federal Maritime Commission. *Hawaiian Trade Study: An Economic Analysis*. Government Printing Office, 1978. |
| **An interview you conducted** | Brandt, Deborah. Personal interview. 28 May 2008.<br><br>(Note: List the interview under the name of the interviewee) |
| **A film/DVD** | Note: This depends on the focus of your Work. Please see the MLA Style blog for a detailed explanation. |
| **A Page on a Website with no author** | "Stunning Lakeside View on Lake Erie." *VisitPA,* Commonwealth of Pennsylvania, 7 |

| | |
|---|---|
| | June 2018, www.visitpa.com/article/stunning-lakeside-views-lake-erie. |
| **A Page on a Website with an author** | Del Castillo, Inigo. "How Not to Kill Your Houseplants, According to Botanists." *Apartment Therapy,* 29 Jan. 2020, www.apartmenttherapy.com/houseplant-tips-botanists-36710191. |
| **Artwork - from website** | Sherald, Amy. *Former First Lady, Michelle Obama.* 2018. *National Portrait Gallery,* npg.si.edu/object/npg_NPG.2018.15. |

**(Source: Official Chicago Manual website cited in the University of Pittsburg. (2020). Citation Styles: APA, MLA, Chicago, Turabian, IEEE: MLA 8th Edition. https://pitt.libguides.com/citationhelp/mla8thedition (Accessed, Friday, July 31, 2020)**

## Citing and Referencing Electronic Sources in APA, MLA, and Numerical (CHICAGO, NALT, OSCOLA)

In these days of information and communication technology (ICT), the internet and other electronic sources have become vital sources of information for researchers. All a researcher has to do to get desired information from the internet, for example, is to type into the search engine, the right keywords. Some popular search engines include Google, Bing. Yahoo. Baidu, Yandex, Duckduckgo, Contextual Web Search and Yippy Search (RapidAPI, 2020)

Thus, electronic sources are quick, accessible, and easy to use. Their importance notwithstanding, researchers often have difficulty citing and referencing them. This difficulty is mainly because some electronic sources lack authors, dates and may have web addresses that are too long.

As in the case with other referencing styles, there should also be a link between citation and the full reference in the case of electronic sources. In effect, what appears in the citation, for example, a name or a number, will connect with the full reference entry. (Neville, 2010)

### Citing and Referencing Advertisements

Media practitioners, as well as those in marketing, find advertising very useful. When advertisement materials are used in an academic paper, Neville (2010:58) listed what should be in the reference as follows:

- Name(s) of the creators of the advertisement. This might be a named person, agency, or company, organization or institution promoting the goods or services concerned
- Year of origin of the advertisement, if known. If not known, but 'c' or 'circa' and an approximate decade, e.g. (circa the 1930s)
- Title of the advertisement, or description of product/service
- Nature of the advertisement, e.g. [Radio advertisement]
- Name (and description, if necessary) of the host for the advertisement
- The date you heard or saw it, and time, if applicable
- Page number, if applicable.

## Table 6- Citing and Referencing Adverts

| HARVARD | APA |
|---|---|
| VISIT Malam Bala (2009). Bala currency converter: N1 equals £1. (Advertisement). 'The Observer Magazine,' 10 June 2020, p.35. | Visit Malam Bala (2020, June 10). Bala currency converter: N1 equals £1Advertisement]. 'The Daily Trust,' p.35. |
| **MLA** | **NUMERICAL (Chicago, OSCOLA, NALT)** |
| Visit Malam Bala. "Bala Currency Converter: N1 Equals £1." Advert. 10 May 2009, Daily Trust, 35. | VISIT MALAM BALA. *Bala currency converter:£1 equals £1* (Advertisement). 'The Daily Trust,' 10 June 2020, p.35. |

## NALT System of Citation and Referencing

The dearth of a uniform citation style for legal studies in Nigeria spurred the Nigerian Association of Law Teachers [NALT] to come up with the NALT referencing manual, called the Greenbook in 2016. Notwithstanding dearth of uniformity in citation styles, the footnote method, as opposed to the in-text and endnote methods, is the mostly applied in citing sources in legal research reports.

The NALT system of referencing is an easy-to-use and follow citation template which is recommended for law research writings in law faculties in Nigerian Universities. According to the NALT Manual of Style, the Greenbook (2018):

> NALT Uniform Citation Guides adopt 'Footnotes' style of referencing, whereby Arabic numerals are used (in superscripts) in the body of the essay to identify sources of document consulted, or the issues sought to be clarified and emphasised. This means that every source cited must be reflected at the foot of each page (with Arabic numeral-1, 2, 3...) to see at a glance, all information concerning the sources referred to with the Arabic numeral in the text.

## NALT's Specimen for Footnotes Citation Referencing

### 1. Books-

a) Give the name of the author the exact way it appears on the publication. Leave out prefixes, eg professor, Mr, Dr etc. Thus, Professor Olufemi Abifarin, Commercial Law in Nigeria, when cited in a footnote will be: Olufemi Abifarin, Commercial Law in Nigeria, Iyamho: (EUI Publishers, 2020) p.25
b) For Three authors- insert "and" between their names. Example: F. Masajuwa, S. Imoisi and I. Edetalehn, *Elements of Contract Law in Nigeria* (1st edn, EUI Publishers, 2020) p.8
c) Three authors and above: Give the details of the first author followed by "and others" Example: O.A. Odojor and others, The *Fundamentals of Family Law in Nigeria.* (Spectrum Books, 2019)
d) Chapter in a book: Example: Florence Masajuwa' Ethnicity and Class in Nigeria' in Akin Oshuntokun, David Aworawo and Florence Masajuwa (Eds.) *History and Cultures of Nigeria Up to A.D. 2000* (Malthouse, 2003): 265 -280

### 2. Journals, Example: Umukoro, Nathaniel. 'Democracy and inequality in Nigeria' (2014) (30) (1) *Journal of Developing Societies*, 1-24.

### 3. Online Journals: Follow this format.

| Author | Title | year | Volume/issue | *Journal's name/Abr.* | Web Address | Date Accessed |
|---|---|---|---|---|---|---|

Example: Florence Masajuwa, 'Beyond Ogoni Clean-Up: Rethinking Environmental Protection Laws Governing the Operation of the Oil Industry in Nigeria' 2020, 10 (1) *Petroleum Technology Development Journal* [PTDJ] https://www.ptdjournal.com/?page_id=8 accessed 1st August 2020.

### 4. Newspapers, Magazines etc.

Onus Ashely, 'The Role of Class Representatives in Nigeria's Tertiary Institutions' The Nigerian Observer May 4, 2020, p.10

Magazine- Freedom Atigbi, 'Scrap NDDC Now' Tell Magazine, 27th July -2nd August, 2020, p. 3

### 5. Cases

| *Case name* | Year | Court | Number | Year | volume | Report Abbreviation | First Page | |
|---|---|---|---|---|---|---|---|---|

Example: Italicize the name of the case. Lower case letter "v" should be used to separate the names of the parties in the case. Only the names of the case should appear in-text. The citations of the case should go to the footnote, the year the decision was handed down should be stated in square brackets. Provide specific information regarding where the case was published, for example in a law report, and the page is also provided. The abbreviation of the court which gave the decision is also stated (Solomon, 2017:13).

*Abacha v Fawehinmi* [2000] FWLR (Pt. 4) 533,

Cite foreign cases in the manner it is cited in the home jurisdiction (University of Oxford, 2012: 32 as cited in Solomon, 2017). Eg. Kesavananda (n 1) 241-252.

### 6. Citation of the Constitution of the Federal Republic of Nigeria

In the first instance, it should be cited in full, with the word "amended" attached to it. This mode of citation is used exclusively for the Constitution of the Federal Republic of Nigeria 1999. Subsequently, it may be cited by way of the acronym, CFRN 1999 (as amended), or by some descriptions, for instance, the "1999 Constitution."

### 7. Citation of Statutes:

Cite them in the short titles often as indicated in the enacted law itself. Also, cite the chapter under which the statute is arranged.

Examples: i) The Evidence Act, 2011, cap 50; ii) The Administration of Criminal Justice Act, 2015, the Petroleum Act, 1969.

### 8. Citing Unpublished Works-Dissertations, Thesis,

Example: K. Ekwere, 'Sustainable Development of Oil and Gas in the Niger Delta: Legal and Political Issues' (Ph. D dissertation, Law of the Sea and Maritime Law Institute, University of Hamburg 2009) p. 66. (Solomon, 2017)

### OSCOLA Citation and Referencing System

The Oxford University Standard for Citation of Legal Authorities [OSCOLA] is currently in its 4th Edition since 2012. It is edited by the Oxford Law Faculty, in consultation with the OSCOLA Editorial Advisory Board. (Faculty of Law, University of Oxford, 2012). According to the initiators of the OSCOLA style, "OSCOLA style is designed to facilitate accurate citation of authorities, legislation, and other legal materials." It is thus, widely used in law schools and by journal and book publishers in the U.K. and beyond.

OSCOLA is a footnote style: all citations appear in footnotes. OSCOLA does not use endnotes or in-text citations. When citing any source, either directly (as a quotation) or indirectly (by paraphrasing or referring to ideas in a source), cite the reference in a footnote, in the style indicated in OSCOLA. This segment gives examples of how to cite the following:

1. Cases
2. Legislation
3. Book
4. Chapters in edited books
5. Journal articles and
6. Web pages and blogs

**Examples of the OSCOLA Style**

**Steps to Footnote**

**1.** Indicate footnotes with a superscript number which should appear after any relevant punctuation in the text. (University of Strachlide Library Guide, 2020)

Example: The National Gender Policy has not improved the quality of gender relations in Nigeria.[1]

**2. (a) Put the footnote marker at the end of a sentence**. (Wiley, 2020)

**Example:**

The government should use all means to end insurgency so that these displaced women can return to their ancestral communities.[4]

**(b) Where the note is meant for specific emphasis, then it is necessary to put it directly after the word or phrase to which it relates.**

**Example:** The regulatory authorities of law programmes[5] do generally not support MCQ as only a method of examination for law students.

### 3. Close footnotes with a full stop.

Example: Dire Living Conditions in Nigeria's Capital for Thousands who Escaped Boko Haram Attacks in the Northeast, *Aljazeera,* (Abuja, 26 March 2018).

### 4. Where more than one citation is given in a single footnote reference, separate them with semi-colons.

**Example:** Recent cases have raised questions about the extent of executive power and its relationship to parliamentary sovereignty.[15] However, this does not mean that... (OSCOLA, 4th Ed., 2012).

When dropped at the foot of the paper as a footnote, this is what [15] represents:

15 Cherry v Advocate General [2019] CSIH 49, 2019 SLT 1097; R (on the application of Miller) v Prime Minister [2019] UKSC 41, [2020] AC 373.

### 5. OSCOLA section 1.2 dwelt on Subsequent citations under the footnoting style

According to the University of Pittsburg Library (2020),

If you cite a source and then cite it again later in your Work, you need not cite the source in full in each subsequent citation. You can 'briefly identify the source and provide a cross-citation to the footnote in which the full citation can be found.' This cross-citation would be in the form (n 3) - where 'n' indicates 'note' and '3' is the number of the footnote - so the reader looks at footnote 3 to find the full citation.

If the subsequent citation is in the footnote immediately following the full citation, you can use 'ibid' instead.

Examples:

3 *Cherry v Advocate General* [2019] CSIH 49, 2019 SLT 1097.

4 ibid [53]–[60] (Lord Carloway). (University of Pittsburg, 2020)

12 Cherry (n 3).

For more detail on how to indicate subsequent citations, see section 1.2.1 of OSCOLA, 4th edn as cited in the University of Pittsburg Library publication, 2020

## 6. Making and Citing Quotations

i. Up to three lines: You should incorporate quotations of up to three lines into the text within single quotation marks:

Lord Carloway described this period of prorogation as 'an extraordinary length of time.'[27]

Quotations within short quotations have double quotation marks round them ("...").

ii. Longer than three lines: Quotations of more than three lines should be presented in an indented paragraph.

**Example:**

On participation in decision making by IDPs, Ladan (2015) argued thus:

The Kampala Convention ("K.C.") under Article 9(2) k places an obligation on State Parties not only to consult IDPs but also to allow them to participate in decisions relating to their protection and assistance including public participation under Article 9(2) L of same K.C. in democratic governance. In order to realize this obligation, countries are enjoined to create mechanisms or channels through which IDPs can participate in decision making whose outcomes will affect their lives.

## Table 7: OSCOLA Citation and Referencing Style

| LEGAL MATERIAL | EXAMPLES |
|---|---|
| **CASES** | 1). Give the party names, followed by the neutral citation, followed by the *Law Reports* citation (eg A.C., Ch, QB, *Dangana & Anor. v Usman & 4 Ors* [2012] 2 S.C. (Pt. III) 103).<br>2). To cite a specific part of a judgment with numbered paragraphs, include the paragraph number(s) in the footnote citations, e.g.: Anderson v Imrie [2018] CSIH 79, 2019 SC 243 [3]<br>Williams v Hackney LBC [2018] UKSC 37, [2019] AC 421 [62]–[69]<br>3). To cite a specific part of a judgment with no numbered paragraphs, include the page number(s) in the footnote citations, e.g.: R v Leeds County Court, ex p Morris [1990] QB 523 (Q.B.) 530–31 |
| **LEGISLATIONS** | 1). Constitution of the Federal Republic of Nigeria 1999 (as amended) Cap. C23 Laws of the Federation of Nigeria 2004 (CFRN, 1999) s. 4.<br>2). CFRN, 1999, s. 12(1). |
| **BOOKS**<br><br>**Encyclopedias**<br>Halsbury's Laws (5th edn, 2010) vol 57, para 53 | Give the author's name in the same form as in the publication, except in bibliographies, where you should give only the surname followed by the initial(s). Give relevant information about editions, translators and so forth before the publisher, and give page numbers at the end of the citation, after the brackets. EXAMPLES: Thomas Hobbes, Leviathan (first published 1651, Penguin 1985) 268; Charles Lipson. Cite right: a quick guide to citation styles--MLA, APA, Chicago, the sciences, professions, and more. (University of Chicago Press, 2011).<br>Give the Edition if the book as indicated in the book. EXAMPLE: Edwina Higgins and Laura Tatham, Successful Legal Writing (3rd edn, Sweet & Maxwell 2015) |
| **CHAPTER IN BOOK** | Example: Yinka Omorogbe, Y. 'The legal framework for public participation in decision- |

| | making on mining and energy development in Nigeria: giving voices to the voiceless.' in Donald N. Zillman, Alastair R. Lucas & George (Rock) Pring, eds., Human rights in natural resource development: Public participation in the sustainable development of mining and energy resources. (Oxford University Press, 2002) |
|---|---|
| **JOURNAL PAPERS:**<br>**1) Hard copy** | **1). Hard copy**: Paul Craig, 'Theory, "Pure Theory" and Values in Public Law' [2005] PL 440<br>2). Soft Copy (online): Alabi, R.A "Comparative Analysis of Socio-Economic Constraints in Niger-Delta." European Journal of Economics, Finance and Administrative Sciences.10,(2008),63–74: <http://eurojournals.com/ejefas10.pdf#page=63> |
| **WEB PAGE /BLOGS** | Example: Chioma Unini, 'Coalition Writes Buhari, Lists 14 High Profile Corruption Cases Against AGF, Malami' (The Nigerian Lawyer, 3 August, 2020) <https://thenigerialawyer.com/coalition-writes-buhari-lists-14-high-profile-corruption-cases-against-agf-malami/> accessed 3 August 2020. |
| **NEWSPAPERS** | **Example:** Osaretin Osadebamwen, 'Order Buhari to Publish Details of Govt Loans since 2015, SERAP Tasks Court' (Abuja, 3 November 2020) 1 |

**Source: The chapter writer**

## Reference Management Tools

Reference management tools are also referred to as 'citation management software' or 'bibliographic software' or 'personal bibliographic file managers (Praharaj, 2016). They are softwares that help researchers and writers manage citations and referencing at the snap of the fingers or at a click of a mouse! According to Fenner, Scheliga & Bartling (2014: 126) "A reference manager is a software package that allows scientific authors to collect, organize, and use bibliographic references or citations." Also, a good number of reference software offer opportunities to organise references into folders and subfolders. A few others allow the inclusion of full-text-papers in PDF format (ibid).

The idea of a reference manager and the accompanying tools came in the wake of current information and communication technology (ICT) era. There are many of them, and all a researcher need to do is select the type most suitable to the researcher's needs (Mahajan et al, 2013). While a number of these tools are web-based to facilitate collaboration among researchers, some of them can be stored and used in mobile devices. Besides, most institutions of learning have one or more of these referencing management software installed in their libraries for mutual use of staff and students. While some are paid for, others are free for users online. The most known of these referencing tools include Endnote, Mendeley, Zotero, Citationsy, and RefWorks.

**Endnote**

Endnote is a reference management software package produced by Thomson Reuters (Fenner et al, 2014). It has been around for over 20 years and is a top-rated reference management tool for collaborative research with colleagues anywhere in the world. EndNote Online and EndNote Desktop also enable one to import references into ones work, allowing one to 'cite while writing,' so that they appear as citations in the main text and as references in the reference list/bibliography.

Another highlight of Endnote is that it includes reference types such as interviews, podcasts, conference papers, and press releases. It also lets one add citations to Microsoft PowerPoint slides (ibid).

**Table 8- Summary of the Highlights of Selected Reference Management Tools**

| Reference management software | Cost | Does it integrate with Microsoft Word? | Can it capture a webpage to create a record? |
|---|---|---|---|
| RefWorks | US$100/year or free at any subscribing academic institution | Yes (requires download of Write-N-Cite utility) | Yes |
| Zotero | Free/open source | Yes (also works with OpenOffice) | Yes |
| EndNote | US$249.95 | Yes (also works with OpenOffice) | No |
| Mendeley | Free | Yes (also works with OpenOffice) | Yes |
| Citationsy | Free | Yes (also works with OpenOffice) | Yes |

**Source: Scribendi. (n.d). Up Close: The 5 Best Reference Management Programs. Available at https://www.scribendi.com/academy/articles/reference_management_software_solutions.en.html (Accessed, Tuesday, August 11, 2020)**

## Mendeley

Mendeley has both a desktop and a web version. Elsevier acquired this tool in early 2014 from a London based startup that developed it. Some of the highlights of this tool include having networking and collaborative features and also providing facilities for efficiently managing PDF files (Chukwu, 2017).

## Zotero

Zotero is both free and open-source which was originally developed as a plugin for the Firefox browser. The newer Zotero Standalone offers the same functionality but runs as a separate program and works with Firefox, Chrome, and Safari. There is a hosted version of Zotero used to synchronize references across devices as well as share them in private or public groups (Fenner et al, 2014). Zotero is a great choice as a reference manager for researchers and students because it runs as both a web service and an offline service on all personal devices such as laptop, iPad, cell phone, etc. (Scribendi, n.d). It automatically and seamlessly extracts information from books, journal articles, and other online sources, making the entire process of creating a reference list effortless.

## Citationsy

Citationsy is very adaptable. This adaptability is because it can be accessed as a page within a browser. It can also be downloaded as a chrome extension or mobile app. In effect, one can access one's library from any device with an internet connection. One does not need to manually type citations as this tool automatically extracts the citation details, just like other reference tools. This software can also be used to scan the barcodes of texbooks refered to in the paper (Scribendi.com).

## RefWorks

RefWorks is web-based and paid for through subscription. It developed and owned by ProQuest. This software can be used to format manuscripts in various ways. Refwork is also useful in managing other data outside bibliographic data (Scribendi, n.d). Another feature is that the "Write N Cite" utility enables the integration of references into Microsoft Word, where in-text citations and reference lists can be formatted into various styles. Another feature of RefWorks is that it stores all cited sources online for secure collaboration. Thus, weak or unstable internet services hinder this tool from functioning well. Offline usage of RefWorks is possible, this is however, not very effective.

## Conclusion

This chapter examined the various citations and referencing styles that are currently in use in the humanities, social sciences, management, and legal studies. The essence is to acquaint researchers and academic writers in these fields with the current trends in the use of the avalanche of information and materials out there online and offline. The referencing styles were developed by various academic and professional bodies to meet their own unique referencing needs. Thus, each referencing method is as useful or relevant as the other. The techniques can be classified into two main types: the author (name)-date style and the footnote style. To lessen the time spent gathering references for materials sourced online, some organisations developed reference management tools such as Mendely, Endnote, Zotero, etc. These tools are handy and available online for free or for a fee. In these days of ICT, it is expedient that academic writers and researchers become knowledgeable about how to deploy these research enhancing tools in their writings.

In all, a writer only needs to know the style best suited for the kind of academic paper he or she is writing. Quite often, agencies offering platforms for publishing research findings inform prospective contributors to the preferred citation and referencing styles of the agency.

## References


The American Psychological Association. (2020). *Publication Manual*. (7th ed.). American Psychological Association.

Bachelorprint. (nd).Academic writing: Referencing and citation styles. Retrieved, Monday, July 20, 2020 from https://www.bachelorprint.eu/academic-writing/referencing-citation-styles.

Bryson, D. (2012). Using research papers: citations, referencing and plagiarism. *Journal of visual communication in medicine*, *35*(2), 82-84.

Chukwu, S. (2017). Using Mendely Referencing Management Software to Organize Your Research Citations/References. A Paper Presented on Modern Tools for Citation and Referencing for Postgraduate Students of Federal University of Technology, Owerri on 25th January, 2017

Lipson, C. (2011). *Cite right: A quick guide to citation styles--MLA, APA, Chicago, the sciences, professions, and more*. University of Chicago Press.

Longman Dictionary. (2020). Available at www. https://www.ldoceonline.com/dictionary/style.Accesed Monday, July 20, 2020

Mahajan, A. K., & Hogarth, D. K. (2013). Taking control of your digital library: how modern citation managers do more than just referencing. *Chest*, *144*(6), 1930-1933.

Moore, S., Neville, C., & Murphy, M. (2010). *The ultimate study skills handbook*. McGraw-Hill Education (U.K.).

Neville, C. (2010). The complete guide to referencing and avoiding plagiarism. (2nd Edition) Open University Press.

OSCOLA Referencing Style Retrieved Monday, July 6, 2020 from https://www.law.ox.ac.uk/research-subject-groups/publications/oscola

Praharaj, S. K. (2016). Citing and referencing in research papers. *Kerala J Psychiatry*, *29*, 74-8.

RapidAPI. (2020).Top 8 Best Search Engines of 2020). Retrieved, Wednesday, July 29, 2020

Retrieved Friday, 10April 2020 from at www.apa.org/books.

Scribendi. (2020). Up Close: The 5 Best Reference Management Programs. Available at https://www.scribendi.com/academy/articles/reference_management_software_solutions.en.html (Accessed, Sunday, July 12, 2020)

Solomon, E. (2017). Towards Effective Legal Writing in Nigeria. *Journal of Commonwealth Law and Legal Education, 12*(1).

University of Chicago Press. (2017). *Chicago Manual of Style*. University of Chicago Press. Retrieved Thursday, 9 April, 2020 from https://www.chicagomanualofstyle.org/home.html

University of Kent, (2012). Academic Integrity. Retrieved Sunday, July 12, 2020 from https://www.kent.ac.uk/ai/students/whatisreferencing.

University of Leeds Library. (2017). Academic Integrity. Retrieved Monday, 6 July, 2020 from https://library.leeds.ac.uk/info/1401/academic_skills/46/academic_integrity_and_plagiarism.

University of Oregon Remote Law Library Services.(2020). - Remote law library services. Retrieved Friday 12 June, 2020 from https://researchguides.uoregon.edu/lawremote.

University of Queensland. (2020). Referencing style guides. Retrieved Sunday, July 12, 2020 from https://guides.library.uq.edu.au/referencing

University of Strachlide. (2020). Referencing: OSCOLA (Law). Retrieved Thursday, 30 JULY, 2020 from https://guides.lib.strath.ac.uk/referencing_guide/referencing/oscola.

Williams, A. (2013). *Research: Improve your reading and referencing skills (Collins Academic Skills)*. HarperCollins U.K.